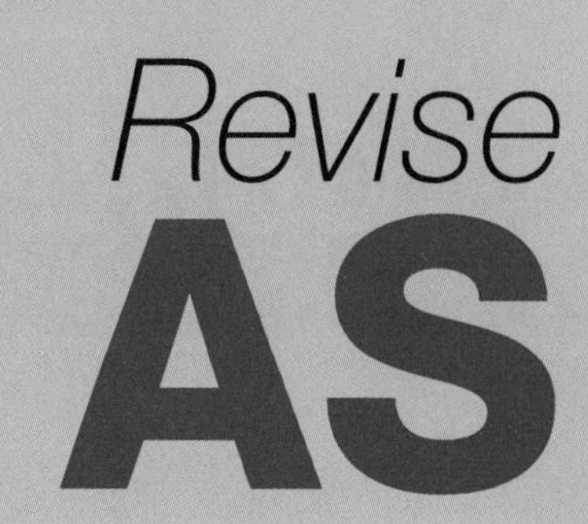

English Literature

Margaret Walker

Contents

Chapter 4 Pre-twentieth-century prose

Chapter 5 Twentieth century prose

Chapter 6 Drama

Specification lists

Here is a list of the different specifications for English Literature at AS Level. The choice of specification does not depend on you, of course, but you can see from this the details of what you will be studying.

Note that there are two AQA specifications, A and B.

AQA A English Literature

MODULE	SPECIFICATION TOPIC	CHAPTER REFERENCE	STUDIED IN CLASS	REVISED	PRACTICE QUESTIONS
Unit 1 The Modern Novel	*The Spire: William Golding*	*5*			
	Cold Mountain: Charles Frazier	*5*			
	Possession: A.S. Byatt	*5*			
	Wise Children: Angela Carter	*5*			
	Spies: Michael Frayn	*5*			
Unit 2 *Shakespeare in context/ coursework*	*Richard II*	*1, 2*			
	The Tempest	*1, 2*			
	Much Ado About Nothing	*1, 2*			
Unit 3 *Drama/ Poetry*	*The School For Scandal: Richard Brinsley Sheridan*	*6*			
	'Tis Pity She's a Whore: John Ford	*6*			
	A Woman of No Importance: Oscar Wilde	*6*			
	Comedians: Trevor Griffiths	*6*			
	Making History: Brian Friel	*6*			
	All My Sons: Arthur Miller	*6*			
	Beowulf: Seamus Heaney	*6*			
	The Miller's Prologue and Tale: Geoffrey Chaucer	*3*			
	Selected Poems: Thomas Hardy	*3*			
	Selected Poems of the Brontës	*3*			
	High Windows: Philip Larkin	*3*			
	The World's Wife: Carol Ann Duffy	*3*			

Examination analysis

Unit 1	*I question*	*I hour (closed text)*	*30%*
Unit 2	*Either: a) One question closed text* *Or: b) Coursework I or 2 essays 1500 words*		*30%*
Unit 3	*2 questions*	*2 hours (open text) one text must be pre-I900*	*40%*

AQA B English Literature

MODULE	SPECIFICATION TOPIC	CHAPTER REFERENCE	STUDIED IN CLASS	REVISED	PRACTICE QUESTIONS
Unit 1 Novel	*The Color Purple: Alice Walker*	4			
	Tess of the D'Urbervilles: Thomas Hardy	4			
	Great Expectations: Charles Dickens	4			
	Waterland: Graham Swift	5			
	Pride and Prejudice: Jane Austen	5			
	The Great Gatsby: F. Scott Fitzgerald	5			
	The God of Small Things: Arundhati Roy	5			
Unit 2 Drama/ Poetry (pre-1900)	*The Death of a Salesman: Arthur Miller*	6			
	Selected Poems: John Keats	6			
	Amadeus: Peter Shaffer	6			
	Top Girls: Caryl Churchill	6			
	Look Back In Anger: John Osborne	6			
	A Shropshire Lad: A.E. Housman	6			
	The Miller's Tale: Geoffrey Chaucer	3			
	Selected Poems: John Donne	3			
	Paradise Lost Book 1: John Milton	3			
	Songs of Innocence and Experience: William Blake	3			
	Cat on a Hot Tin Roof: Tennessee Williams	3			
	Rosencrantz and Guildenstern are Dead: Tom Stoppard	3			
Unit 3 Shakespeare in context/ coursework	*Coursework: no set text*				

Examination analysis

Unit 1	*1 question*	*1 hour 15 mins (open text)*	*30%*
Unit 2	*2 questions*	*1 hour 45 mins (closed text)*	*40%*
Unit 3	*Either: a) One question open text* *Or: b) Coursework 1 or 2 essays 1500 words*		*30%*

Edexcel English Literature

MODULE	SPECIFICATION TOPIC	CHAPTER REFERENCE	STUDIED IN CLASS	REVISED	PRACTICE QUESTIONS
Unit 1 Drama/ poetry	a) The Rover: Aphra Behn	6			
	Translations: Brian Friel	6			
	Top Girls: Caryl Churchill	6			
	Professional Foul: Tom Stoppard	6			
	A Streetcar Named Desire: Tennessee Williams	6			
	b) Edexcel Anthology	3			
	Letters from a Far Country (from 'Collected Poems'): Gillian Clarke	3			
	Best of Betjeman: John Betjeman	3			
	Selected Poems: John Keats	3			
	Penguin Book of American Verse	3			
Unit 2 Pre-1900 Prose	Return of the Native: Thomas Hardy	4			
	Frankenstein: Mary Shelley	4			
	Emma: Jane Austen	4			
	Hard Times: Charles Dickens	4			
	Washington Square: Henry James	4			
Unit 3 Shakespeare in context exam/ coursework	Henry V	1, 2			
	Much Ado About Nothing	1, 2			
	The Winter's Tale	1, 2			
	Hamlet	1, 2			
	Antony and Cleopatra	1, 2			

Examination analysis

Unit 1	2 questions	2 hours (open text)	40%
Unit 2	1 question	1 hour (closed text)	30%
Unit 3	Either: a) 1 question open text Or: b) Coursework 1 or 2 essays 1500 words		30%

OCR English Literature

MODULE	SPECIFICATION TOPIC	CHAPTER REFERENCE	STUDIED IN CLASS	REVISED	PRACTICE QUESTIONS
Unit 1 Shakespeare	*Henry IV pt 2*	1, 2			
	As You Like It	1, 2			
	Antony and Cleopatra	1, 2			
	The Tempest	1, 2			
Unit 2 Poetry and Prose	*Dracula: Bram Stoker*	3			
	The Franklin's Tale: Geoffrey Chaucer	3			
	Selected Poems: Tony Harrison	3			
	Selected Poems: T.S. Eliot	3			
	Complete Sonnets: William Shakespeare	3			
	Selected Poems: Byron	3			
	Granny Scarecrow: Anne Stevenson	3			
	Selected Poems: Edward Thomas	3			
	Selected Poems: Robert Browning	3			
	Persuasion: Jane Austen	4			
	Heart of Darkness: Joseph Conrad	4			
	A History of the World in 10½ Chapters: Julian Barnes	4			
	Jane Eyre: Charlotte Brontë	4			
	Mary Barton: Elizabeth Gaskell	5			
	Short Cuts: Raymond Carver	5			
	A Passage to India: E.M. Forster	5			
Unit 3	*Coursework: prose, poetry and drama*	3, 4, 5, 6			

Examination analysis

Unit 1	*1 question* *either one or two plays; 1 passage based, 1 essay based*	*1 hour (closed book)*	*30%*
Unit 2	*2 questions*	*2 hours (open text) one text pre-1900*	*40%*
Unit 3	*Either: a) piece of creative/recreative writing with commentary and text based essay* *Or: b) two essays (prose, poetry or drama) 3000 words*		*40%*

WJEC English Literature

MODULE	SPECIFICATION TOPIC	CHAPTER REFERENCE	STUDIED IN CLASS	REVISED	PRACTICE QUESTIONS
Unit 1 Shakespeare	*King Lear*	1, 2			
	Measure for Measure	1, 2			
	Richard II	1, 2			
	The Merry Wives of Windsor	1, 2			
Unit 2 20th century prose/poetry /drama	*Regeneration: Pat Barker*	5			
	A Toy Epic: Emyr Humphries	5			
	Selected Poems: W.B. Yeats	3			
	Selected Poems: Dylan Thomas	3			
	Translations: Brian Friel	6			
	Death of a Salesman: Arthur Miller	6			
Unit 3 20th century poetry/ pre-1900 prose	*Selected Poems: Ted Hughes*	3			
	Selected Poems: Eavan Boland	3			
	Welsh Retrospective: Dannie Abse	3			
	Selected Poems: Carol Ann Duffy	3			
	Selected Poems: Seamus Heaney	3			
	The Picture of Dorian Gray: Oscar Wilde	3			
	Emma: Jane Austen	3			
	The Mayor of Casterbridge: Thomas Hardy	3			
	The Mill on the Floss: George Eliot	3			
	The Awakening and other stories: Kate Chopin	3			

Examination analysis

Unit 1	*1 question*	*1 hour (closed text)*	*30%*
Unit 2	*Either: a) 1 question* *Or: b) Coursework approved text*	*1 hour (open text)* *1500–2000 words*	*30%*
Unit 3	*2 questions*	*2 hours (open text)*	*40%*

NICCEA English Literature

MODULE	SPECIFICATION TOPIC	CHAPTER REFERENCE	STUDIED IN CLASS	REVISED	PRACTICE QUESTIONS
Unit 1 Poetry after 1800/ 20th century drama	*Selected Poems: Emily Dickinson*	3			
	Selected Poems: Robert Frost	3			
	Opened Ground: Seamus Heaney	3			
	Selected Poems: Gerard Manley Hopkins	3			
	Selected Poems: Stevie Smith	3			
	Selected Poems: Edward Thomas	3			
	Selected Poems: W.B. Yeats	3			
	A Man for All Seasons: Robert Bolt	6			
	Making History: Brian Friel	6			
	Glengarry Glen Ross: David Mamet	6			
	Betrayal: Harold Pinter	6			
	Observe the Sons of Ulster Marching Towards the Somme: Frank McGuinness	6			
	Amadeus: Peter Shaffer	6			
	A Streetcar Named Desire: Tennessee Williams	6			
Unit 2 Shakespeare	*Richard II*	1, 2			
	As You Like It	1, 2			
	King Lear	1, 2			
	Coriolanus	1, 2			
	The Tempest	1, 2			
Unit 3 Pre-20th century prose	*The Gothic novel*	4			
	The rise of the novel	4			
	The Victorian novel	4			
	The Irish 'Big House' novel	4			
	Nineteenth-century American fiction	4			

Examination analysis

Unit 1	*1 question from each section*	*2 hours (open text)*	*40%*
Unit 2	*1 question*	*1 hour (closed text)*	*30%*
Unit 3	*Coursework; one assignment of about 1500 words*		*30%*

AS/A2 Level English Literature courses

AS and A2

All English Literature Literature courses being studied from September 2000 are in two parts, with three separate units or modules in each part. Most students will start by studying the AS (Advanced Subsidiary) course. Some then go on to study the second part of the A Level course, called the A2. It is also possible to study the full A Level course, both AS and A2 at the same time.

How will you be tested?

Assessment units

For AS English Literature, you will be tested by three assessment units. For the full A Level in English Literature, you will take a further three units. AS English Literature forms 50% of the assessment weighting for the full A Level.

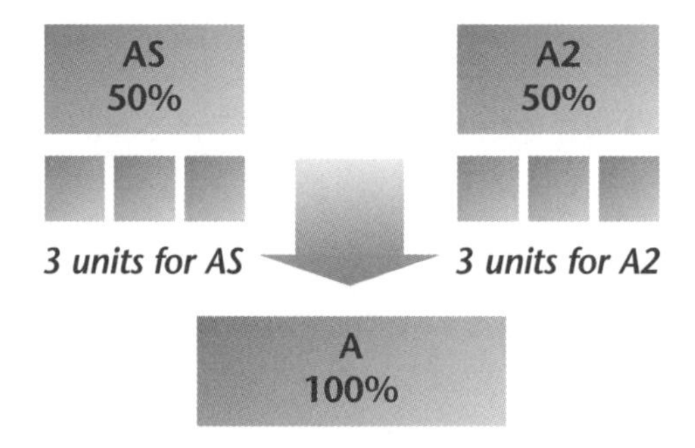

Each unit can normally be taken in either January or June. Alternatively, you can study the whole course before taking any of the unit tests. There is a lot of flexibility about when exams can be taken and the diagram below shows just some of the ways that the assessment units may be taken for AS and A Level English Literature.

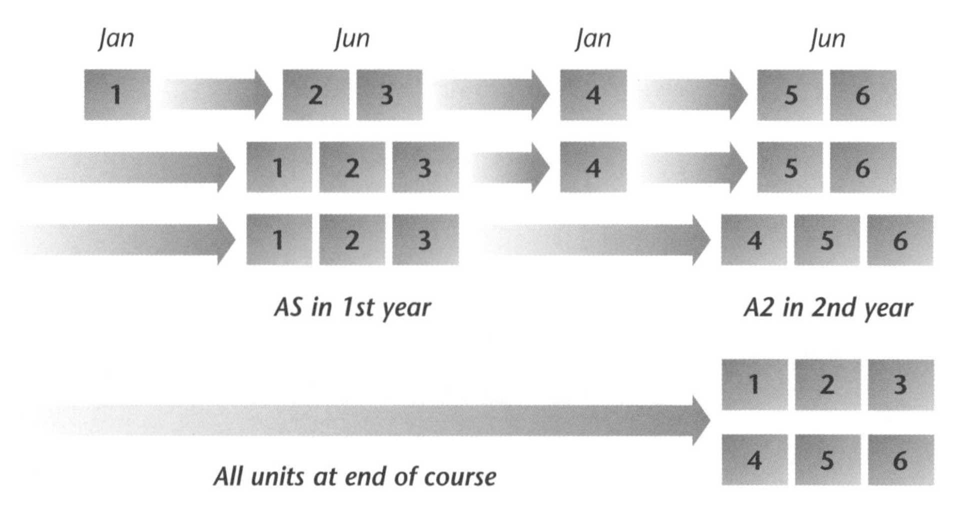

If you are disappointed with a module result, you can resit each module.

A2 and Synoptic assessment

For those students who having studied AS decide to go on to study A2, there are three further units to be studied. One unit draws together all the skills and objectives of the course in a 'synoptic' assessment.

Coursework

Coursework (internally assessed work) may form part of your A Level English Literature Literature course, depending on which specification you study. The form and length of the coursework varies, and may include one or two pieces of work, including the possibility of creative as well as analytical writing.

Key skills

It is important that you develop your key skills throughout the AS and A2 courses that you take, as these are skills that you need whatever you do beyond AS and A Levels. To gain the key skills qualification, which is equivalent to an AS Level, you will need to demonstrate that you have attained Level 3 in Communication, Application of number and Information technology. Part of the assessment can be done as normal class activity and part is by formal test. It is a worthwhile qualification, as it demonstrates your ability to put across your ideas, collect data and use up to date technology in your work.

What skills will I need?

For AS Level English Literature Literature, you will be tested by *assessment objectives*: these are the skills and abilities that you should have acquired by studying the course. The assessment objectives for AS Level English Literature Literature are shown below.

AOl

Communicate clearly the knowledge, understanding and insight appropriate to literary study, using appropriate terminology and accurate and coherent written expression.

A02i

Respond with knowledge and understanding to literary texts of different types and periods.

A03

Show detailed understanding of the ways in which writers' choices of form, structure and language shape meanings.

A04

Articulate independent opinions and judgements, informed by different interpretations of literary texts by other readers.

A05i

Show understanding of the contexts in which literary texts are written and understood.

These assessment objectives will be tested in every part of the course and questions are written in order to test you on them. They also form the basis of the mark schemes used to decide your final grade.

Exam technique

Links from GCSE

Since there are three different subjects at A Level: English Literature Literature, English Literature Language and English Literature Language and Literature combined, it is possible that you could do two of these as two separate AS or A2 subjects. These two would have to be English Literature Literature and English Literature Language. The combined English Literature cannot be taken as well as any other English Literature subject.

You will find that there are similarities between what you did at GCSE, and what you are asked to do at AS Level, but that the skills required from you at AS are both more demanding, and more varied. So what you have already done is relevant and useful, but you must be prepared to think more about the **context** in which texts are written and interpreted, and about the way writers **present** their ideas. At AS Level, it is not enough to **describe**; you now need to **analyse**.

As you will need to progress from GCSE, so you will find that what you do at AS Level is preparing you for the A2 year, if you choose to carry on your studies in this subject.

Unlike some other AS Level subjects, the emphasis is on **skills** as much as **knowledge** and **understanding**, which is why this book focuses on helping you to develop these skills.

You will all have studied Shakespeare at Key Stage 3 and GCSE, and you will see that all the specifications include the study of at least one Shakespeare play. What you have already learned about Shakespeare's plays will be relevant and helpful for you at the next stage, but you do need to move beyond character and plot at AS Level.

In every unit of your course, no matter which specification you are using, you must show an awareness of **genre**, that is, the **kind** of text you are discussing.

In every chapter and section of this book, you will be encouraged to demonstrate your understanding, and your skills.

What are examiners looking for?

You must be aware of the significance of the assessment objectives. These are referred to in every chapter, and they are crucial to your performance at both AS and A2 Level English Literature Literature. Examiners use the objectives to frame the questions they set for the exam papers, and they are also the basis of the mark schemes. It is very important that you are aware which objectives are being assessed on which paper, since this varies from exam board to exam board, and paper to paper.

You should also be aware of the differences between exams where you take your text in with you, and those where you are not allowed to. The specifications vary in how this is organised, and you need to know how this affects the kinds of questions set, and how to answer them.

In the section of suggested questions and answers, you will find information and advice on this.

You need to remember too that you are assessed not just by exams, but by coursework. It is important that you apply your skills to all aspects of your course. The coursework is testing the same objectives as the exams. Not all centres will choose the coursework option, but many will. Coursework accounts for 30% of the total marks at both AS and A2.

What grade do you want?

Everyone would like to improve their grades but you will only manage this with a lot of hard work and determination. You should have a fair idea of your natural ability and likely grade in English Literature and the hints below offer advice on improving that grade.

There are a number of points to bear in mind:

- stay relevant
- remember which AOs are being tested
- read the question carefully
- construct and sustain an argument
- always give evidence from the text to support your comments
- make sure your written English Literature is as accurate as possible
- use your time properly
- check what you have written
- think before you write
- remember there is no one right answer, but you have to be convincing about your views.

You should find the advice in this book helpful and relevant. Use it wisely: no one can do your thinking, reading and preparing for you!

Four steps to successful revision

Step 1: Understand

- Study the topic to be learned slowly. Make sure you understand the logic or important concepts.
- Mark up the text if necessary – underline, highlight and make notes
- Re-read each paragraph slowly.

GO TO STEP 2

Step 2: Summarise

- Now make your own revision note summary:
  What is the main idea, theme or concept to be learned?
  What are the main points? How does the logic develop?
  Ask questions: Why? How? What next?
- Use bullet points, mind maps, patterned notes.
- Link ideas with mnemonics, mind maps, crazy stories.
- Note the title and date of the revision notes
  (e.g. English Literature: Shakespeare, 3rd March).
- Organise your notes carefully and keep them in a file.

This is now in short term memory. You will forget 80% of it if you do not go to Step 3.
GO TO STEP 3, but first take a 10 minute break.

Step 3: Memorise

- Take 25 minute learning 'bites' with 5 minute breaks.
- After each 5 minute break test yourself:
  Cover the original revision note summary
  Write down the main points
  Speak out loud (record on tape)
  Tell someone else
  Repeat many times.

The material is well on its way to long term memory.
You will forget 40% if you do not do step 4. GO TO STEP 4

Step 4: Track/Review

- Create a Revision Diary (one A4 page per day).
- Make a revision plan for the topic, e.g. 1 day later, 1 week later, 1 month later.
- Record your revision in your Revision Diary, e.g.
  English Literature: Shakespeare, 3rd March 25 minutes
  English Literature: Shakespeare, 5th March 15 minutes
  English Literature: Shakespeare, 3rd April 15 minutes
  ... and then at monthly intervals.

Chapter 1

Shakespeare 1: Dramatic techniques and effects

After studying this chapter you should know about:

LEARNING OBJECTIVES

- *place of assessment; importance of assessment objectives*
- *effects of genre*
- *importance of performance; focus on presentation*
- *dramatic techniques: use of dialogue; opening scenes; ending scenes; distribution of power in the plays; language and images; foreshadowing; juxtaposition; contrasts; pace; moral judgements in the plays*
- *skills: analysis; understanding of form and structure; developing and supporting arguments; asking the right questions; right and wrong approaches*

1.1 Assessment

AQA A	U2
AQA B	U3
EDEXCEL	U3
OCR	U1
WJEC	U1
NICCEA	U2

The assessment of Shakespeare is part of all AS specifications, although the method of assessment varies. Almost everyone sitting A Level English Literature will have already studied at least one Shakespeare play. But an important point to remember is that at A Level you will be assessed in a different way, and with different objectives in mind.

You may have to write about a Shakespeare play (or plays) as part of your coursework, or as your first exam. In either case, you will need to keep in mind that you do have prior knowledge, which you can build on.

No matter which form of assessment is applicable in your case, you will be tested on assessment objective (AO):

1 Your ability **to communicate clearly the knowledge, understanding and insight appropriate to literary study, using appropriate terminology and accurate and coherent written expression.**

Remember that this objective is present in almost every unit that you study. This is the most common objective, so it should affect the way you respond to every part of your AS course.

Another important objective is AO4, which you will remember is the one that requires you to form your own judgements, whilst also responding to other readers' interpretations. You will need to read critical views, but also to discuss with others, including your fellow students.

Assessment objective 5 is targeted here also, particularly in coursework. You need to **show understanding of the contexts in which literary texts are written and understood**. Each of the specifications has additional help in defining and explaining this idea. But it is a crucial one.

Coursework

The different exam boards offer you an almost free choice of texts if your Shakespeare unit is internally assessed. The word limits vary from 1500 to 3000 words, and you may be asked to write one essay or two. Edexcel requires you to study one of 5 plays if you choose the coursework option: *Antony and Cleopatra, Hamlet, Henry V, Much Ado About Nothing, The Winter's Tale.*

Set texts for OCR. *Henry IV part 2 Othello, Antony and Cleopatra, As You Like It, The Tempest.*

For WJEC: *King Lear, Measure for Measure, Richard II, The Merry Wives of Windsor.*

AQA A's set plays (for exam) are: *The Tempest, Richard II, Much Ado About Nothing.*

NICCEA set plays (for exam) are: *Richard II, As You Like It, King Lear, Coriolanus, The Tempest.*

Edexcel set plays (for exam) are: *Henry V, Antony and Cleopatra, The Winter's Tale, Much Ado About Nothing, Hamlet.*

Exam

For two boards, WJEC and OCR, your response to Shakespeare is assessed by exam. There is no choice within the specification, and for both boards, the exam is closed text, which means that you cannot take your copy of the play into the exam with you. For most candidates, this will imply a different approach to study and assessment. For both AQA A and Edexcel, the alternative to coursework is a one-hour open text exam. For AQA B, only coursework is available.

In the following section you will be looking at ways of writing about Shakespeare in order to fulfil the different assessment objectives. The ideas, terminology and approaches are appropriate and relevant to both external (exam) and internal (coursework) assessment of Shakespeare.

1.2 Genre

AQA A U2
AQA B U3
EDEXCEL U3
OCR U1
WJEC U1
NICCEA U2

When you are writing about any text, it is important that you are aware of the effects of the **genre**. Shakespeare writes plays, not novels or poems, and therefore any exam or coursework essay you write should be based on an understanding of the way the genre, or type of writing, works.

The concept that Shakespeare writes for the stage, and not the reader, is central to an informed response to his plays.

KEY CONCEPT

Here are some of the features you need to bear in mind when you think about the **performance** of a play:

- conflict
- contrasts
- changes
- tension
- suspense
- juxtaposition
- revelations
- secrets
- variety
- pace
- movement
- humour
- key moments
- symbolism
- pauses and silences
- distribution of power

We will be referring to these ideas in this and the following chapter, along with other key concepts.

You need to bear in mind that every performance is an interpretation. There can be no one performance that is a definitive one. That is why it is useful to watch as many versions as possible of the plays you are studying. Read reviews too, because they will help you to discover how plays are interpreted and how critics have responded to the interpretations. And of course all the time you are reaching the assessment objective about your own and other people's interpretations.

1.3 Particular techniques and effects

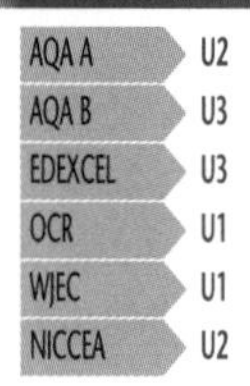

During the course of this chapter we will examine the ways in which Shakespeare uses these dramatic techniques, and analyse their effects, always in the light of the fact that we are talking about plays which are meant to be performed.

Any assignments that you write on Shakespeare should be based on the following:

- awareness of dramatic techniques and effects, and that Shakespeare is purposefully creating and structuring his plays
- an informed response to the context of the plays
- an awareness of different interpretations of the plays.

By responding to this idea, you are targeting AOs 1, 2i and 3.

1.4 Opening scenes

AQA A	U2
AQA B	U3
EDEXCEL	U3
OCR	U1
WJEC	U1
NICCEA	U2

The Winter's Tale

Read the following carefully. It is the opening scene from *The Winter's Tale.*

This discussion of the opening scene of the play has as its purpose a focus on dramatic techniques and presentation. It includes key words which will be explained in their context, and returned to in other discussions.

Although this discussion is based on a particular play, the ideas are relevant to other plays by Shakespeare and other dramatists.

Enter Camillo and Archidamus

ARCHIDAMUS If you shall chance, Camillo, to visit Bohemia, on the like occasion whereon my services are now on foot, you shall see, as I have said, great difference betwixt our Bohemia and your Sicilia.

CAMILLO I think this coming summer the King of Sicilia means to pay Bohemia the visitation which he justly owes him.

ARCHIDAMUS Wherein our entertainment shall shame us: we will be justified in our loves. For indeed –

CAMILLO Beseech you –

His language is exaggerated?

ARCHIDAMUS Verily, I speak it in the freedom of my knowledge: we cannot with such magnificence, in so rare – I know not what to say. We will give you sleepy drinks, that your senses, unintelligent of our insufficience, may, though they cannot praise us, as little accuse us.

CAMILLO You pay a great deal too dear for what's given freely.

ARCHIDAMUS Believe me, I speak as my understanding instructs me and as mine honesty puts it to utterance.

Look how these images work together.

CAMILLO Sicilia cannot show himself over-kind to Bohemia. They were <u>trained</u> together in their childhoods; and there <u>rooted</u> betwixt them then such an affection, which cannot choose but <u>branch</u> now. Since their more mature dignities and royal necessities made separation of their society, their encounters, though not personal, hath been royally attorneyed with interchange of gifts, letters, loving embassies: that they have seemed to be together, though absent; shook hands as over a vast; and embraced, as it were, from the ends of opposed winds. The heavens continue their loves!

Does this make audience feel apprehensive?

ARCHIDAMUS <u>I think there is not in the world either malice or matter to alter it.</u> You have an unspeakable comfort of your young prince Mamillius. It is a gentleman of the greatest promise that ever came into my note.

Note images which fit together.

CAMILLO I very well agree with you in the hopes of him. It is a gallant child; one that indeed <u>physics</u> the subject, makes old hearts fresh. They that went on <u>crutches</u> ere he was born desire yet their life to see him a man.

ARCHIDAMUS Would they else be content to die?

CAMILLO Yes – if there were no other excuse why they should desire to live.

ARCHIDAMUS If the King had no son, they would desire to live on crutches till he had one.

It doesn't matter whether you are familiar with the play or not. This is an opening scene and the playwright's task is to make the audience intrigued, involved and informed. Read it through, and think about the following points:

- Who are these people?
- What kind of situation is this?
- What relationship do these men have to the kings they are talking about?
- Why is the audience seeing things through their eyes?
- What kind of language are they using?
- What kind of mood is established here?
- Is the audience given hints of any possible problems or developments?

Response/commentary

Here are some thoughts about this scene that will help you when you look at any opening scene.

The speech is extremely sophisticated. Although the scene is in prose, not verse, these two men are obviously cultured and very polite. Their sentences are balanced and even weighty, but they do seem to have some difficulty in getting to the point. They talk about the friendship of two kings which suggests the sort of social sphere they are in. The court setting seems perhaps unnatural in spite of the natural **images** Camillo uses when he refers to the kings being 'trained together' in their childhood, and of their 'rooted affection' which must 'branch now'.

What we learn

The audience is being given valuable information here which is needed in order to make sense of the rest of the play. It is always worth registering what you learn from an opening scene, and how you learn it. You pick up ideas, moods and a sense of the power relations in the world you are being introduced to.

For one thing, you might like to think about Archidamus's declaration that nothing will alter the king's affection: 'I think there is not in the world either malice or matter to alter it.' The audience should now be alert to the possibility of alteration even though this has been denied.

How we might feel

There is a distinct sense of **foreshadowing** here. That is, a feeling of uneasiness, perhaps because of the undesirability of denying the gods or fate. If you know the play, you will also know that the following scene very quickly disrupts this apparent equilibrium. If you don't know the play, you may still experience some sense of unease, an awareness of the effects of the **connotations**, or associations, of particular words or groups of words, without being able yet to realise their full significance. You can form an impression of the **ideas** and **images** which will be important in the play.

Characters

It is useful to realise when you read on from an opening scene of a play to think about the characters who appear again and in what role. Archidamus never appears again and seems only to serve the purpose of being someone for Camillo to talk to. But Camillo goes on to play an important role in the play, being forced to make a difficult and painful decision in the first act.

Relationships

In fact, relationships themselves seem to be a focus in this opening scene. You could pick out the references to friendship, to childhood and to nature as significant. You could note the images of sickness and cure: 'physic' and 'crutches', for example. You can also see that the audience is being given the long view, with references to the childhood of the two kings, their present (the visit of the king of Bohemia to his friend, the king of Sicilia) and the future when the young prince will be a man.

General effects

You could usefully compare this opening scene to that of the play you are studying. Think about the way that Shakespeare, the dramatist, **presents** the world of the play. It is important that you don't think about character as you may have done during your GCSE study, but rather about the **presentation** of character in the larger world created and **structured** by the writer.

If you don't know the play, you will still be able to grasp something of the situation which Shakespeare is creating and presenting. It's important to look at what follows any scene. In this case the audience is immediately introduced to the two kings who have just been discussed. One effect of the opening scene, then, is to focus attention on the relationship of these two men, so that the audience will be alert to any possible changes and developments. Since conflict is the essence of drama, Shakespeare has suggested possible future areas of difficulty by having the two opening characters stress the lack of conflict. So the audience awaits future **plot** developments. The **presentation** and **juxtaposition** (placing together) of the two scenes immediately shapes the audience's response. A writer gains effects by placing one scene, one character next to one another.

KEY CONCEPTS

ambiguity	conflict	connotations	construction
context	contrast	dialogue	foreshadowing
form	ideas	images	interaction
juxtaposition	moral values	plot	power
presentation	rhythm	structure	tension

Possible question format

Your tasks might well include an analysis of a particular scene or scenes, perhaps in the context of the play as a whole. All these are possible ways of framing questions, and show the focus on dramatic presentation which is so important.

- How dramatically convincing and effective do you find this scene?
- Compare key speeches with other speeches.
- How important is this scene in the context of the play as a whole?
- Have you any sympathy for the characters?
- By means of specific reference to speeches of your own choice, explore the ways in which Shakespeare contrasts this setting with that setting.
- Using (extract) as your starting point, examine the ways in which Shakespeare effectively conveys both feelings and ideas in the play.
- Is ______ a suitable hero for this play?
- What part do ______ and ______ play in the themes and structure of the play as a whole?
- In Act 1 ______ says '…'. But in Act 5, he says '…'. Examine the changes in his ideas and attitudes, the reasons for these changes and the ways that his language reflects this.
- Analyse Shakespeare's presentation of the relationship between ______ and ______ and evaluate its importance in the play as a whole.
- Remind yourself of Act ______ scene ______ from ______ to ______ .
  Explore the importance of ______ 's role here, and analyse Shakespeare's presentation of her in the play as a whole.
- Explore the dramatic significance of ______ in this play.
- Choose two parts of the play which you think are of great dramatic effectiveness and importance. Analyse them to show how Shakespeare achieves his effects.
- What feelings are you left with at the end of the play, and why?
- Choose two extracts from the play which show conflict of some kind. Examine how this conflict is presented.
- Are the women stronger than the men in this play?

King Lear

Contrast the opening of another play, King lear. Think about the key concepts on page 19.

By saying this, isn't the audience going to suspect the opposite?

These words are linked by sound.

Images of coining.

KENT I thought the King had more affected the Duke of Albany than Cornwall.

GLOUCESTER It did always seem so to us, but now in the division of the kingdoms it appears not which of the Dukes he values most, for equalities are so weighted that curiosity in neither can make choice of either's moiety

KENT Is this not your son, my lord?

GLOUCESTER His breeding, sir hath been at my charge. I have so often blushed to acknowledge him that I am now brazed to it.

KENT I cannot conceive you.

GLOUCESTER Sir, this young fellow's mother could, whereupon she grew round-wombed and had, indeed, a son for her cradle ere she had a husband for a bed. Do you smell a fault?

KENT I cannot wish the fault undone, the issue of it being so proper.

GLOUCESTER But I have, sir, a son by order of law. Some year elder than this, who is yet no dearer in my account. Though this knave came somewhat saucily into the world before he was sent for, yet was his mother fair, there was good sport at his making, and the whoreson must be acknowledged. [To Edmund] Do you know this noble gentleman, Edmund?

EDMUND No, my lord.

GLOUCESTER My lord of Kent. Remember him hereafter as my honourable friend.

EDMUND [To Kent] My services to your lordship.

KENT I must love you, and sue to know you better.

EDMUND Sir, I shall study deserving.

GLOUCESTER [To Kent] He hath been out nine years, and away he shall again.

Sound a sennet

The king is coming.

Discussion

Unlike the previous opening, both Gloucester and Kent here go on to play important roles in the rest of the play. We start in the middle of the action with the discussion of what seems to be a contentious and competitive issue. It appears that the kingdom is being divided, and that the king has favourites. It seems to place the country in a most unstable situation, though Kent and Gloucester soon move on to discuss other topics. Undoubtedly, however, we will return to this instability.

What Gloucester has to say about Edmund could also be tied in to the notion of a kingdom being divided. Gloucester tells Kent, and the audience, that Edmund is his illegitimate son. The language he uses to reveal this perhaps strikes us as unsuitable, given that Edmund is standing there with him. The terms he uses to describe Edmund's mother seem particularly inappropriate as he refers to the 'good sport' of his 'making', and Edmund himself is referred to as 'this knave' and 'whoreson'. The pun on 'conceive' is in dubious taste in the circumstances. Gloucester's tone here is a bit like someone boasting in a pub about his sexual conquests, and he tells Kent that he is 'braz'd' to admitting Edmund's existence. He is, in other words, no longer embarrassed by his illegitimacy. What's more, he compares Edmund to his older, legitimate, son 'who is no yet dearer in my account'.

We can see a number of significant ideas in this brief exchange. The two older men are clearly from the higher ranks of society, and they enjoy a comfortable relationship with one another, using informal prose as their medium of communication. Kent is named 'my lord of Kent'. They are familiar with events of the courts, though neither of them was right about whom the king was favouring, a situation which is apparently changeable.

Edmund has little to say in this extract. This is a lot to do with relative status, of course: he is the younger and illegitimate son, which means that he has no possibility of inheritance, and no title. But his presence might suggest potential for future events. Can he take this conversation about his mother, his birth, his brother and his appearance ('proper') without some kind of reaction? The figure of Edmund suggests, then, dramatic potential, as well as raising issues of inheritance, family relationships and power, and the position of women, and men's attitudes towards them.

When you place this against [juxtapose] the information about the division of the kingdom, this might suggest that we are in the midst of a society in which established order, both of the kingdom and the family, is moving towards being broken down. And all this has emerged form a very brief exchange. The fact that the king is about to enter, to continue the process of dividing his lands will yoke these ideas together more firmly.

Hamlet

Now let's look at the opening scene of *Hamlet*. Take some time now to read the following extract in the light of the comments on the previous opening scenes. See what **comparisons** and **contrasts** you can note. You might usefully compare this opening scene to any that you are familiar with.

Enter Francisco and Barnardo, the two sentinels

BARNARDO Who's there?

FRANCISCO Nay, answer me. Stand, and unfold yourself

BARNARDO Long live the king!

FRANCISCO (Barnado?)

BARNARDO (He)

FRANCISCO You come most carefully upon your hour.

BARNARDO 'Tis now struck twelve. Get thee to bed, Francisco,

FRANCISCO For this relief much thanks. 'Tis bitter cold,
And I am sick at heart

BARNARDO (Have you had quiet guards?)

FRANCISCO Not a mouse stirring.

BARNARDO (Well, good night.)
If you do meet Horatio and Marcellus,
The rivals of my watch, bid them make haste.

FRANCISCO I think I hear them. Stand ho! Who is there?

HORATIO (Friends to this ground)

MARCELLUS And liegemen to the Dane.

FRANCISCO (Give you good night.)

MARCELLUS O, farewell, honest soldier.
Who hath relieved you?

FRANCISCO Barnardo hath my place.
Give you good night.

MARCELLUS Holla, Barnardo!

BARNARDO What, is Horatio there?

HORATIO A piece of him.

BARNARDO Welcome, Horatio. Welcome, good Marcellus.

MARCELLUS What, has this thing appeared again tonight?

BARNARDO I have seen nothing.

MARCELLUS Horatio says 'tis but our fantasy
And will not let belief take hold of him
Touching this dreadful sight twice seen of us.
Therefore I have entreated him along
With us to watch the minutes of this night,
That, if again this apparition come,
He may approve our eyes and speak to it.

HORATIO Tush tush, 'twill not appear.

BARNARDO (Sit down awhile,)
And let us once again assail your ears,
That are so fortified against our story,
What we have two nights seen.

HORATIO (Well, sit we down,)
And let us hear Barnardo speak of this.

BARNARDO Last night of all,
When yond same star that's westward from the pole
Had made his course t'illumine that part of heaven
Where now it bums. Marcellus and myself
The bell then beating one –

Enter the Ghost

MARCELLUS Peace, break thee off. Look – where it comes again.

BARNARDO In the same figure like the King that's dead.

MARCELLUS Thou art a scholar. Speak to it, Horatio.

BARNARDO Looks 'anot like the King? Mark it Horatio.

HORATIO Most like. It harrows me with fear and wonder.

BARNARDO It would be spoke to.

MARCELLUS Speak to it, Horatio.

Discussion

Language, form and structure

Here we have an extract from a much longer scene and the atmosphere has little in common with the previous ones. Now the audience is aware of **tension** and of uncertainty. Look at the ways in which the men challenge one another. There is darkness and some confusion; we do not yet know who is who. But Shakespeare's dramatic skill enables him to manipulate the situation so that we are given vital information: Horatio is there, it seems as a sceptical observer. The men seem edgy and jumpy. The **rhythm** of the lines helps to convey this to us. The lines must be spoken quickly and with little pause for reflection. And notice the way in which one speaker completes another's line. This technique is always suggestive of haste, tension or lack of ease. The men are aware of a situation which we as the audience have to deduce piece by piece. We are led to speculate about the Ghost and we become part of this atmosphere of uncertainty in which there seems to be difficulty in establishing the truth. We have, however, acquired a good deal of essential background information during the course of the scene, but in a natural way, in that we seem to be part of this uneasy and tense group of men. Unwittingly, we have become drawn in to the world of *Hamlet*.

Look back and compare again these opening scenes to consolidate your understanding of Shakespeare's dramatic techniques.

1.5 Endings

AQA A	U2
AQA B	U3
EDEXCEL	U3
OCR	U1
WJEC	U1
NICCEA	U2

It would be useful at this point to think about the ending of a play, to get the sense of the dramatist's technique. Read the extract below from *King Lear* and ask yourself the following question: What feelings are you left with as you finish reading the play? This is a question you can ask yourself about the play you are studying, since it's an important part of what we can think about when we study any kind of literature.

King Lear, Act 5, scene 3, lines 270 to 301

[In this part of the scene, the aged King Lear is holding the dead body of his youngest daughter, Cordelia.]

ALBANY You lords and noble friends, know our intent.
What comfort to this great decay may come
Shall be applied; for us, we will resign
During the life of this old majesty
To him our absolute power;
[*To* EDGAR *and* KENT] you to your rights,
With boot and such addition as your honours
Have more than merited. All friends shall taste
The wages of their virtue, and all foes
The cup of their deservings. - O see, see!
LEAR And my poor fool is hanged. No, no, no life?
Why should a dog, a horse, a rat have life,
And thou no breath at all? Thou'lt come no more.
Never, never, never, never, never.
[*To* KENT] Pray you, undo this button. Thank you, sir.
Do you see this? Look on her. Look, her lips.
Look there, look there. *He dies*
EDGAR He faints. [*To* LEAR] My lord, my lord!
KENT [to LEAR] Break, heart, I prithee break.
EDGAR [to LEAR] Look up, my lord.
KENT Vex not his ghost. O, let him pass. He hates him
That would upon the rack of this tough world
Stretch him out longer.
EDGAR He is gone indeed.
KENT The wonder is he hath endured so long.
He but usurped his life.
ALBANY Bear them from hence. Our present business
Is general woe. [*To* EDGAR *and* KENT] Friends of my soul, you twain
Rule in this realm, and the gored state sustain.
KENT I have a journey, sir, shortly to go;
My master calls me; I must not say no.
ALBANY The weight of this sad time we must obey,
Speak what we feel, not what we ought to say.
The oldest hath borne most. We that are young
Shall never see so much, nor live so long.

Discussion

Many students when writing about the ending of a tragedy, repeat what they have at some point read or been told about this genre, even when it bears no relationship to the play they have studied.

Characters in tragedies don't meet their fate because of a 'fatal flaw': it's not an appropriate comment about Shakespearean tragedy. It's all so much more complicated than that. They die because of the society they live in, because of the situation they are in, because of moral duties and responsibilities placed upon them, because of political events, as well as because of choices they have made. It is also not true to suggest that at the ending of a tragedy all the loose ends have been tied up, and that society can continue in a better way, as if a wound or illness has been healed. Look at the ending of King Lear, above. The old king dies, not merely because of foolish choices he made, but because of others' ambitions and weaknesses, as well as because of the changing and unstable world he lived in. And he is not the only one to die: his three daughters die, as well as some of his loyal retainers. One of his daughters, Cordelia, is innocent of any wrong doing. Her death seems completely arbitrary.

The rhyming couplets at the end of the play certainly give a sense of rounding off, but not of completion in a satisfactory way. It's hard to imagine audiences going home after a performance of this play feeling that all is resolved nicely. Some characters seem to be punished way beyond anything they have deserved. The sheer injustice of this is reflected in Lear's heartbreaking words. Look at the effect of the repetition of the word 'never'. The finality of this is what strikes us, and the unfairness of a world in which 'a dog, a horse, a rat' can live, but not Cordelia.

Albany wanted to restore power to Lear, and to ensure that all got what they deserved:

All friends shall taste
The wages of their virtue, and all foes
The cup of their deservings.

But this is not what happens. Lear is overtaken by the greatest of tragedies. The only consolation, some critics have argued, is that he dies apparently believing that she still lives. Kent is not prepared to 'rule in this realm', the 'gored state'. He has 'a journey' as his 'master calls him'. Like Lear, he is ready to die. This is a world in which all have suffered, but 'the oldest have borne most'. As Edgar says, it is important to 'speak what we feel, not what we ought to say'. Students often argue in their exam answers that everything is returned to normal at the end of a tragedy, such as King Lear, Hamlet or Othello, but you should think about the ways in which Shakespeare stresses what has been lost or damaged during the course of the play. As always, look at the words on the page, and if possible at the actions on stage in forming your own judgement about the impact of the ending of a play.

1.6 Dialogue

AQA A	U3
AQA B	U3
EDEXCEL	U3
OCR	U1
WJEC	U1
NICCEA	U2

The dialogue in the plays is, of course, of great importance. We will be examining dialogue in the plays from various points of view, but for the moment, we will concentrate on one extract from *The Winter's Tale*.

The Winter's Tale

In this extract, Florizel, prince of Bohemia, has fallen in love with Perdita whom he thinks of as a shepherd's daughter. She is in fact the lost daughter of Leontes, King of Sicilia, but this is not revealed until the last act. This scene (IV. iv), in which Florizel is disguised as a rustic himself for the sheep-shearing festival, is thus full of dramatic ironies, in which the audience knows more than any of the characters. It is well worth bearing this in mind when you read a play: think about where you are situated in comparison with the characters on stage. You probably know more than they do: your position is usually privileged. Read through this extract and make notes on the language that the two characters use, and what this reveals about their relationship.

Enter Florizel and Perdita

FLORIZEL These your unusual weeds to each part of you
Does give a life: no shepherdess, but Flora
Peering in April's front. This your sheep-shearing
Is as a meeting of the petty gods,
And you the queen on't.

PERDITA Sir, my gracious lord,
To chide at your extremes it not becomes me –
O, pardon that I name them: your high self,
The gracious mark o'th'land, you have obscured
With a swain's wearing, and me, poor lowly maid,
Most goddess-like pranked up. But that our feasts
In every mess have folly, and the feeders
Digest it with accustom, I should blush
To see you so attired, swoon, I think,
To show myself a glass.

FLORIZEL I bless the time
When my good falcon made her flight across
Thy father's ground.

PERDITA Now Jove afford you cause!
To me the difference forges dread; your greatness
Hath not been used to fear. Even now I tremble
To think your father by some accident
Should pass this way, as you did. O, the Fates!
How would he look to see his work, so noble,
Vilely bound up? What would he say? Or how
Should I, in these my borrowed flaunts, behold
The sternness of his presence?

FLORIZEL Apprehend
Nothing but jollity. The gods themselves,
Humbling their deities to love, have taken
The shapes of beasts upon them: Jupiter
Became a bull, and bellowed; the green Neptune
A ram and bleated; and the fire-robed god,
Golden Apollo, a poor humble swain,
As I seem now. Their transformations
Were never for a piece of beauty rarer.
Nor in a way so chaste, since my desires

Run not before mine honour, nor my lusts
Burn hotter than my faith.

PERDITA O, but sir,
Your resolution cannot hold when 'tis
Opposed, as it must be, by th'power of the King.
One of these two must be necessities,
Which then will speak: that you must change this purpose
Or I my life.

FLORIZEL Thou dearest Perdita,
With these forced thoughts, I prithee, darken not
The mirth o'th'feast. Or I'll be thine, my fair,
Or not my father's. For I cannot be
Mine own, nor anything to any, if
I be not thine. To this I am most constant,
Though destiny say no. Be merry, gentle;
Strangle such thoughts as these with anything
That you behold the while. Your guests are coming:
Lift up your countenance as it were the day
Of celebration of that nuptial which
We two have sworn shall come.

PERDITA O lady Fortune,
Stand you auspicious!

Commentary

In this scene, we can see that Florizel is presented to us as an impetuous lover, with all the confidence that his rank provides. He undoubtedly loves Perdita, and announces his love forcefully and sometimes tenderly. Look at the speech which begins 'Apprehend/Nothing but jollity': isn't he inclined to ride roughshod over her fears and objections? You can also see both characters refer to the gods. This play is one in which there is no clear-cut religious standpoint. There are both Christian and pre-Christian allusions and references. But here you can see that Florizel uses the gods as comparisons for his own behaviour. He refers to the transformations which gods underwent in order to be with mortal women. And since his motives are so much more chaste than theirs, there is nothing bad or immoral about his intentions. He clearly sees their actions as a possible parallel to his own, which tells us something about his estimation of his own value. He tries to reassure Perdita, to calm her fears.

How successful do you think he is?

Think about your response to that question. It's easy to be carried along by his force, persuasion and impetuosity. But look closely and you can see that Perdita's attitude is less confident. Even Florizel's powers of persuasion cannot talk her round. She has referred to herself as 'poor lowly maid',/ Most goddess-like pranked up'. She seems to suggest that they may be riding for a fall, that their happiness can only be temporary.

What differences between Perdita's and Florizel's attitude do you see here?

She is very conscious of the 'difference' between them, and although her speeches include references to the gods, she also refers to the Fates and 'lady Fortune', implying that far from seeing herself as equal to gods and goddesses, she truly believes in her own inferiority to them: she is after all, merely 'pranked up' but not the real thing. She considers herself at the mercy of the Fates or Fortune. There is no sense that she could defy Fate, but this defiance of Fate, of society's views and of his love for her characterise Florizel's speech and actions. We can see parallels here to Florizel's responses and behaviour in the play as a whole. This defiance also provides a way of distinguishing between other characters in the whole play. But what we should not do is attempt to read a kind of psychological realism in the characters. It's easy to be misled into thinking that 'character studies' have a part to play in your study of A Level English Literature, but it is important to remember that here we must focus on the **presentation** of these **constructs**, for that, after all, is what they are. They reflect the crafting of the writer, but they do not have a life of their own, however convincingly the playwright has given us the illusion of reality. The conclusions we can draw from this extract go beyond the literal meaning, and beyond searching around for thematic significance. Instead we can explore the way that the **dialogue presents** the characters and their relationships to us.

Here we are examining **power** in the play and our own assumptions also, and we are getting a real sense of dramatic **interactions**. Our reading is going beyond the superficial, and incorporating a sense of audience awareness.

1.7 Soliloquies

The word 'soliloquy' comes from Latin and means talking alone. Many students assume that there is only one function of the soliloquy, to show a character engaging in reflection and introspection. But be wary of making this as a blanket statement: soliloquies can serve different purposes in a play. Sometimes, a character is conveying information, or involving the audience in their plans, almost boasting about their own cleverness at times:

Iago in *Othello* uses his soliloquies to inform the audience about his plans and intentions, but also to draw them in. he speaks as if he is actually using these speeches to formulate his plans:

> Make the Moor thank me, love me, and reward me
> For making him egregiously an ass,
> And practising upon his peace and quiet
> Even to madness. 'Tis here but yet confused.
> Knavery's plain face is never seen till used.

The rhyming couplets at the end of this soliloquy give a summing up to the thoughts and plans within the speech. When Iago says "tis here' the actor will very probably point to his head, suggesting that he is creating plans of villainy as he speaks.

Of course, the way that the soliloquies are performed affects their impact on the audience. Several critics argued that the 1981 BBC video production reduced its impact by the way that the soliloquies were directed: Bob Hoskins as Iago spoke them very quietly, almost muttering at times. In this way the scale of the play, and its effects, was reduced. To help in your own interpretation of the play [AO4] think about how you would suggest that these speeches should be delivered.

In *The Winter's Tale* Time acts as a Chorus, giving vital information to the audience, explaining that sixteen years have gone by, and informing them where the action is now set. But Time also serves to create an atmosphere as well as pass on information. The fairy tale aspects of the text are stressed several times during the play, and Time acts as a kind of distancing device. He addresses the audience directly and reminds them that this is constructed, and that they are present at an entertainment.

> Of this allow,
> If ever you have spent time worse ere now;
> If never, yet that Time himself doth say
> He wishes earnestly you never may.

Some characters use soliloquies to explain their dilemmas: Camillo in *The Winter's Tale* has been placed in an impossible situation by his master, King Leontes who, in the grip of a completely unjustified suspicion about his wife, orders him to kill Polixenes, the king's old friend. Crucial to the placing of this speech is the isolation of Camillo: he has no other character to whom he can explain his difficulties, severe as they are. Therefore his soliloquy is a means of expressing his anxieties.:

> O miserable lady! But, for me,
> What case stand I in? I must be the poisoner
> Of good Polixenes, and my ground to do't
> Is the obedience to a master - one
> Who, in rebellion with himself, will have
> All that are his so too.

The conflict may of course be internal, with a character using the form of the soliloquy to tease out ideas, fears or hopes. The crucial aspect of the soliloquy is that the character is alone, that it isn't possible to envisage the speech being delivered to another character in the play. Ask yourself why this is so. You need to examine it within the context of the play, see what part it plays in the text's **structure**.

Many, perhaps most, people would name *Hamlet* as the source of the most famous soliloquies, including, of course, possibly the most famous of all, the 'To be or not to be' speech. The positioning of these soliloquies within the plot of the play is linked to the **structure**, to the way that events are timed and placed, as well as to the developing character of Hamlet, or the audience's developing knowledge of the character. *Hamlet* has been seen by many critics as a play that enquires into the nature of the self, and into the relationship between a human being and their position in society. It is therefore significant that *Hamlet* has several important soliloquies which serve to reveal various philosophical, religious and ethical aspects of the play via Hamlet's reflections.

In the second scene of the play, Hamlet is already contemplating suicide, or rather the religious and ethical implications of suicide:

> O that this too too sullied flesh would melt,
> Thaw, and resolve itself into a dew;
> Or that the Everlasting had not fixed
> His canon 'gainst self-slaughter. O God, God,
> How weary, stale, flat, and unprofitable
> Seem to me all the uses of this world!

The 'canon' is God's law, and Hamlet regrets that suicide is forbidden, since he wishes for his flesh to be dissolved into a 'dew'. All the affairs - 'uses' - of the world mean nothing to him. As well as establishing Hamlet's state of mind, Shakespeare is also indicating the kinds of moral and philosophical questions that are so important in the play.

In a later soliloquy, one in Act 2, Shakespeare uses the technique a little differently. Hamlet comments on his own wordiness:

> Bloody, bawdy villain
> Remorseless, treacherous, lecherous, kindless villain!
> O vengeance!
> Why, what an ass am I! This is most brave,
> That I, the son of a dear father murdered,
> Prompted to my revenge by heaven and hell,
> Must like a whore unpack my heart with words
> And fall a-cursing like a very drab,
> A stallion! Fie upon't, foh!
> About, my brains.

He uses three words which mean prostitute: 'whore', 'drab' and 'stallion'. He berates himself for using words only, and goads himself into better action, telling his 'brains' to get to work. The association between the words and prostitution is unclear; he uses the words as insults to himself from encouragement to a more effective response to his father's murder. He moves for insulting his father's murderer - 'bloody, bawdy villain' - to insulting himself. In a much less serious context, you have probably seen sportsmen doing the same kind of thing. The tone of this soliloquy is quite different from the first one, in its choice of language, and its speed and pace.

One final example from *Hamlet* will demonstrate the versatility and range of Shakespeare's uses of the soliloquy. In Act IV, Hamlet reflects on what might be called the human condition:

> What is a man,
> If is chief good and market of his time
> Be but to sleep and feed? A beast, no more.
> Sure He that made us with such large discourse,
> Looking before and after, gave us not
> That capability and godlike reason
> To fust in us unused.

Hamlet widens the scope of his thought to a consideration of what humanity is capable of, and what a 'man' ought to do. Our intelligence - 'large discourse' - is potentially so great, as is our capacity for reason. These qualities are 'godlike' since God gave them to us, and we are under an obligation to use them, not to let them 'fust', that is, to go mouldy with disuse.

Hamlet is no longer concerned only with himself, his feelings and his situation. He is instead relating his own self and situation to other people and to larger issues, including the relationship between humanity and God.

You need to locate the soliloquy in the context of the play, analysing its purpose as well as its particular features. Don't just assume that there is only one function for the soliloquy, and that all soliloquies are similar in tone and effects.

Bear in mind, also, that where leading characters have very few soliloquies, the audience can't achieve more intimacy with the characters. An example is *Antony and Cleopatra* where we don't find out the motives of the characters by soliloquy. Instead we observe their behaviour, particularly together, and we are perhaps very influenced by the opinions of other characters who frequently comment on their actions, usually unfavourably.

Comedies tend to make less use of the soliloquy than tragedy, but the soliloquy still does play a significant role. Look at Viola's speech from *Twelfth Night*. In a typical comedic convention, Viola is dressed as a boy, a servant, and while she is in love with her 'master', she herself has become the object of the affections of Olivia. Count Orsino, Viola's master has sent her, in her disguise as a young man, Caesario, to woo Olivia on his behalf. The scene is set for a great deal of gender confusion, intensified by the fact that all the female parts would have been played by boys and young men.

> How will this fadge? My master loves her dearly,
> And I, poor monster, fond as much on him,
> And she, mistaken, seems to dote on me:
> What will become of this? As I am man,
> My state is desperate for my master's love;
> As I am woman (now alas the day!)
> What thriftless sighs shall poor Olivia breathe?
> O time, thou must untangle this, not I,
> It is too hard a knot for me t'untie.

Here Viola poses to the audience all the plot complications which it seems impossible to 'untangle'. She wonders how it will 'fadge', that is, work out. The concluding rhyming couplet sums up the idea that events will have to be left to be resolved, that nothing can be done by any one of the characters to sort it all out. The tone is both comical in a rueful way, but also perhaps a little sad. The focus is on gender and disguises, with Viola seeing herself as a 'monster': she is unnatural, being both male and female. All three of these characters seem to be caught in a tangle which no-one can 'untie'. But since this is a comedy, the audience will feel confident that everything will be resolved as happily as possible. This soliloquy gives the audience some indication of Viola's feelings, as well as summing up the narrative complications, and ensuring that they will appreciate the cleverness of the devices which enable a solution to be found.

In *Henry V*, Shakespeare uses the soliloquy spoken by Henry to reflect on the duties and responsibilities of kingship:

> We must bear all. O hard condition,
> Twin-born with greatness, subject to the breath
> Of every fool whose sense no more can feel
> But his own wringing! What infinite heart's ease
> Must kings neglect that private men enjoy!
> And what have kings that privates have not too,
> Save ceremony, save general ceremony?
> And what art thou, thou idol ceremony?
> What kind of god art thou, that suffer'st more
> Of mortal griefs than do thy worshippers?

Henry deliberates on the advantages of kingship, and concludes that they come down to 'ceremony', the symbols of authority and status which a king possesses. But he concludes that these are worth less than the peace of mind which ordinary people -'private men' - enjoy. This soliloquy follows on from a debate the king has with Williams, an ordinary soldier, who stresses the suffering of the common soldiers in war [shown also on page 54]. Kings could expect to be ransomed, not killed. This speech appears to be partly a direct response to this disagreement, with Williams perhaps one of the 'fools' who can only feel their own 'wringing', or pains. Henry stresses the emptiness of the privileges of kingship - the 'idol ceremony'. However, the audience is entitled to wonder if Shakespeare is in fact presenting Henry as attempting to justify himself and his role. He has been seen by many critics as always playing a part, and that the role of king is another such part. His language is ornate, stately and even self-pitying, contrasted to the real feeling of Williams's speech. Although critics and audiences have often responded quite differently to Shakespeare's presentation of Henry in this play, they have all agreed about the central importance of the whole notion of kingship. What they disagree about is the attitudes to kingship within the play.

You do need to bear in mind that it's too easy to write as if these are real characters who are telling the audience what is going on in their 'minds'. Remember that Shakespeare was making use of a well-established convention of the soliloquy as part of the construct that is 'character'. Explore and analyse the uses of the soliloquy within the play you are studying, always linking it to the particular ways it is being used.

All this is part of Shakespeare's **presentation**, that is the methods and techniques used in his plays [AO3], as well as linked to the **form** used within the plays [AO2i].

Summary of skills

What we have examined here has been the way that Shakespeare presents characters to the audience by the way they speak and the way they interact. Through these characters, we can see the working of power, and what ideas and values are underlying the speech. Often what is noticeable is the difficulty of making judgements about behaviour and motives – moral judgements. The plays can often seem ambiguous morally. Because we must always be aware of the importance of genre when studying Shakespeare, we need to keep hold of the idea that these are plays intended to be performed, not novels to be read. But we also need to keep in mind that all performances are interpretations, and there cannot be one performance that gives us the only correct reading.

1.8 What examiners are looking for

AQA A	U2
AQA B	U3
EDEXCEL	U3
OCR	U1
WJEC	U1
NICCEA	U2

Most examiners will tell you that exam candidates don't always do themselves any favours. You need to learn how to apply the skills, knowledge and understanding you have acquired in your course, and apply it to the maximum effect.

Look at the following examples which should help you to understand how best to present your ideas.

Answer A

Text: *Much Ado About Nothing*

Question: Do you agree that in *Much Ado About Nothing* Shakespeare is exploring the role of deception in society?

AOs AO5i is double-weighted for this question, with all the other AOs also being assessed, in equal proportions. This suggests that answers need to include close examination of the idea of 'society' within the play.

Sample question and model answer

1 opinion given, though in very general terms as yet.

2 this is an attempt to give a context, but it's still very general - where is the evidence?

3 where's the evidence?

4 evidence?

5 there is a sense of the whole play, though still not specific

6 Isn't this getting into narrative?

7 asserting this: we still don't have specific textual reference

8 some development perhaps

9 much story telling

10 overview, useful, though nothing is made of it

11 attempt to look at writer's purposes but the concept of 'society' not explored

12 we do need textual support!

13 don't give page references in a play

14 how does he do it? Text!

15 wider reference but still unspecific and undeveloped

16 first quotation!

17 how many times has the student used this phrase? It doesn't sound very literary or confident

18 how? Modern? Why?

I believe that the statement is very true and Act II, scene 1 is a very good example of what Shakespeare is trying to portray [1].

Firstly, we see how popular it was in Shakespearean times [2] to hold masked balls. All the characters in the play very much look forward to the masked ball in Act II, scene 7. They seemed to enjoy the fact that they can hide their identity or indeed make others believe that they were somebody else [3].

At the masked ball Antonio tries to convince Ursula that he is not himself, though she knows full well. [4] This act of deception though harmless could lead to much more, as with Beatrice and Benedick. [5] Benedick pretends that he is not he to Beatrice who then insults Benedick after Benedick denies even knowing the man. [6] Although Beatrice recognises Benedick he doesn't know this. He takes offence and is hurt by Beatrice's words. [7]

In a similar manner, Don Pedro woos Hero for Claudio by pretending to be him. [8] Although his intentions are honourable, Don Pedro is in effect deceiving Hero. Claudio was then deceived by Don John into believing that Don Pedro wanted Hero for himself but this deception was only made possible because Claudio is pretending to be Benedick even though Don John knew his real identity. [9]

In this small portion of the scene we are viewers of at least five acts of deception. One of these acts was motivated by jealousy and therefore meant to do harm while the others though not meant for any bad purpose were still deception or even lies. [10]

I think that in this scene, Shakespeare is showing the audience how society uses deception or lies to manipulate the thoughts of others and also to gain information that they otherwise would not have had if they were honest.11 In the case of Don John, of course, deception was wrong, but I think that Shakespeare is also showing the audience that lies are not always bad and that sometimes it is all right to tell a white lie as long as ones intentions are good. [12]

In Act III, scene 2 (pages 77–78) [13] Don John deceives his brother and Claudio into believing that Hero is unfit to marry Claudio as she is disloyal. 14 This is another of many scenes in which a person or indeed persons are being misled into believing something false. 15 This deception by Don John resulted in the disgrace of Hero who was later publicly accused of not being a 'maid'. [16]

I think [17] that what Shakespeare brings out in this play is how common it was to deceive others in Shakespearean and indeed in modern day society, [18] and the effects, both negative and positive, that this deception could have.

The tone of this answer is distinctly chatty [AO1] and although there is obvious knowledge of the text, there is almost no textual reference and very little sense that it is a play [AO2i]. There is no attempt at all to examine specific details of the play in terms of how it is written [AO3]. There is an argument, but it's often assertive - no evidence again - and very generalised [AO4]. There is some limited attempt to look at context, but the key idea of society is not developed.

Sample question and model answer (continued)

Answer B

Text: *Much Ado About Nothing*

Question: '*In Much Ado About Nothing* Shakespeare shows men as having the real power.' In the light of this view, explore Shakespeare's presentation of the relationships between men and women in *Much Ado About Nothing*.

AOs AO5i is double-weighted for this question, with all the other AOs also being assessed, in equal proportions. This suggests that answers need to include close examination of the idea of gender within the play.

Hero is the embodiment of an upper class lady of Messina. She has been moulded by the expectations and idealisms of men. [1] Beatrice makes a very apt description of her cousin when she says, in response to Antonio asking if Hero will be 'ruled by her father':

Yes faith, it is my cousin's duty to make curtsy and say, 'Father, as it please you'. (II, scene 1)[2]

In the company of men she is quiet and submissive. In the wedding scene, her reaction to Claudio's insinuations are dignified but very submissive. [3] When Claudio talks of his previous pure idea of Hero, [4] she says 'And seemed I ever otherwise to you?' (IV, scene 1, 53). [5].The anger for being falsely accused just is not there. Her being called 'a common stale' is ironic [6] because she is very pure and chaste. When she talks with Margaret just before her wedding, she reveals her fear of losing her virginity: 'for my heart is exceedingly heavy'. [7]

Hero is subjected to horrible cruelty by her betrothed, Claudio, who hurls such insults as 'approved wanton'. Most importantly, he publicly humiliates her, stripping her of dignity. But it is this man that Hero is to marry after the final scene. Hero forgives like the ideal lady. [8]

Margaret, hero's attendant, is crass and unchaste. She is the embodiment of Claudio's idea of Hero when he publicly accuses her. Unlike Hero, she isn't afraid of men. Here she talks to Benedick, not holding back any sexual innuendos: 'Give us the swords, we have bucklers of our own'. [9] We know for certain that she has Borachio as a lover before marriage. Beatrice says to Margaret: 'Ye light o' love, with your heels!' Margaret has a man's licence in speech, such as when she spoke to Benedick, and in her actions. She is the woman men fear. [10]

Benedick's insulting comments on marriage are born out of fear. In particular, he fears cuckoldry and fears the absence of freedom.

Shall I never see a bachelor of threescore again? Go to, i'faith; an thou wilt needs thrust thy neck into a yoke, wear the print of it, and sigh away Sundays. [11]

Claudio also has a great fear of women, or at least real women. Claudio builds up an unrealistic ideal of a woman and applies it to Hero. The irony is that Hero is just such an idealised woman, but the possiblity of her unchastity and sexual corruption makes Claudio panic. Claudio is a social climber, an 'upstart' and his honour is very important. His opinion of Hero is one-dimensional, for she is to him an ornament or a prize.

1 makes a firm statement about character's significance

2 textual support, set out clearly

3 it would be better not to repeat this word

4 could be better expressed

5 support again

6 literary term, correctly and appropriately used

7 support offered, brief and relevant

8 ideas are relevant and opinion comes across, but there could be more development

9 reference to choice and effects of language, but there could be more analysis

10 firm argument, but more development and explanation of this idea would be helpful

11 again useful textual support, but comment on this would assist development of argument

Sample question and model answer (continued)

12 strongly argued and with textual support

13 a very interesting issue, and we could do with hearing more about this

14 the ideas are summarised and concluded

15 an explicit reference to a key word of the question, though there could usefully have been more of this

Beatrice is the feminist of Much Ado About Nothing. She is perhaps the dominant force of her relationship with Benedick. Her hold over Benedick is strong. 'Kill Claudio' is a shocking almost unthinkable request but Benedick by the force of his love for her concedes: [12]

Enough, I am engaged; I will challenge him.

This is very poignant for to break the 'code of honour' whereby there is great solidarity amongst the male allies is unheard of. [13]

The balance of power is almost equal if both these couples are looked at. [14] In Claudio and Hero's relationship, Claudio has the upper hand, the authority. But in the relationship of Beatrice and Benedick, Beatrice, the woman, certainly has the most power. [15]

Discussion

This answer is actually not very much longer than Answer A, but look at how much more ground it covers, and how much more specific reference to the text there is. Not all points in B are fully developed, but there is a real sense of understanding and of focus. The use of terminology is more assured, with the register generally less colloquial, and more grasp of literary language [AO1]. There is much more convincing evidence of knowledge of a range of aspects of the play, though still limited reference to the play's dramatic features [AO2i]. The writer's choices are not given as much attention as the other objectives, though there is a sense of the overall structure of the text and some comment on individual language choice [AO3]. There is much more direction and purpose about the argument [AO4]. Answer B looks more closely at contextual issues, in this case power relations between men and women in the play [AO5i].

Exam practice and analysis

Open Book Question [AQA A]

Much Ado About Nothing

Explore Shakespeare's presentation of loyalty in the play.

Your answer should focus on **not more** than three episodes.

The examining body selects these as the key words:

AO2i: needs understanding of the conventions of the dramatic genre, selecting appropriate scenes, and showing some understanding of attitudes and values.

AO3: focus on presentation here:

- one, two or three episodes
- explore
- presentation
- loyalty
- play

AOs 1, 2, 3 and 4 are assessed in this unit in these proportions: 8%, 10%, 7%. 5%
What distinguishes between a top band and a bottom band answer is the specific focus on these key ideas, with lower band answers describing and narrating, while upper band answers choose appropriate episodes, explore them in close detail and produce a balanced and supported argument.

Chapter 2

Shakespeare 2: More on dramatic techniques and effects

After studying this chapter you should know about:

- *place of assessment; importance of assessment objectives*
- *effects of genre*
- *importance of context*
- *focus on other readers' interpretations*
- *dramatic techniques: presentation of relationships; presentation of character; dramatic structure; roles*
- *skills: analysis; understanding of form and structure; developing and supporting arguments; asking the right questions; right and wrong approaches*

LEARNING OBJECTIVES

2.1 Assessment

AQA A	U3
AQA B	U3
EDEXCEL	U3
OCR	U1
WJEC	U1
NICCEA	U2

In this chapter you will be looking at further assessment objectives, whilst consolidating the knowledge and skills you have already gained. Two AS objectives in particular will be the focus of this chapter:

AO4: Articulate independent opinions and judgements, informed by different interpretations of literary texts by other readers.

AO5: Show understanding of the contexts in which literary texts are written and understood.

ASSESSMENT OBJECTIVES

Reminder

No matter which form of assessment is applicable in your case, you will be tested on AO1: **Your ability to communicate clearly the knowledge, understanding and insight appropriate to literary study, using appropriate terminology and accurate and coherent written expression.**

Remember that this objective is present in almost every unit that you study. This is the most common objective, so it should affect the way you respond to every part of your AS course.

We will also reinforce AO3: **Show detailed understanding of the ways in which writers' choices of form, structure and language shape meanings.**

In this chapter, as in the previous one, you will be looking at ways of writing about Shakespeare in order to fulfil the different assessment objectives. The ideas, terminology and approaches are appropriate and relevant to both external (exam) and internal (coursework) assessment of Shakespeare.

Remember that it is important to stay focused on the idea of **genre** in your study. You must keep a focus on the idea that Shakespeare writes for the stage and not the reader.

2.2 Presentation of 'character'

AQA A	U2
AQA B	U3
EDEXCEL	U3
OCR	U1
WJEC	U1
NICCEA	U2

You should be aware of the importance of a more conceptualised approach to 'character' in the plays. At this point you need to think again about the comments on crafting, and on analysis in the previous chapter. The temptation for you now is to extend what you might have discussed and written about at GCSE, without being aware that you need to consider very carefully your approach to literature. If you had the idea that a writer always has to provide you with a psychologically realistic character which you can identify with (or relate to, as students are so fond of saying!) then you need to change this immediately. This is not the way in to Shakespeare. There is certainly no harm in talking about the plays in this way, but you'll need more than this if you are to be successful in your A Level studies.

The view of Shakespeare's characters which sees them as universal types that we can all recognise may seem an attractive one, but it is actually very restricted and restricting. Shakespeare's characters are often in situations very far from any that we could recognise or see as parallel to our own.

His attention to character varies in different plays; if this is our only criterion of success in drama, we shall have only a partial view of his dramatic achievements. This is not the same as suggesting that we can never expect any explanations for actions, or have any motives offered to us. But the idea of speculating what might be happening between the scenes, as the critic A.C. Bradley, for example, tended to do, is less than helpful. Bradley's critical writings are not a useful model for your own studies. Your attitude to characters may change as the play progresses because of a shift in perspective. Characters may well not be psychologically consistent, and may play different roles during the course of the whole text. The audience may be directed to a different group of characters, for example, as in *The Winter's Tale* where we are not encouraged to identify with any of the characters, and where the action moves from one country to another.

The Winter's Tale

Turn back to the discussion of the opening scene in the previous chapter (page 17). Give yourself a few moments to read back through the scene and remember the comments on it.

Commentary

Think about the fact that we are distanced from the leading Sicilian characters, and given an overview of Leontes, King of Sicilia, his boyhood, his friendship and even his heir, the young prince. If we tried to identify with any of these characters, it would be clear that we would be skewed in our responses to the play as a whole. We would find ourselves attempting to locate a significant psychological core, along with a search for consistent motivation and reactions, when it is in fact much more interesting and useful to examine the **pattern** of the play as a whole.

We can think about how the writer presents characters, and what role these characters play in the text as a whole. If you do this, you are **analysing** not merely describing, or assuming that these characters are real people who have somehow arrived on stage.

Now let's return to the concept of **presentation**. Write down what you think is being asked for by the use of this term.

Progress check

This is not an exhaustive list, but rather points towards research and thinking you can do yourself. If you think about these questions you will realise that you need to dig about in the text when you explore presentation. You are required to demonstrate that you are aware of the author at work; you should be able to show that you can write about a text in a more sophisticated and analytical way than a mere recounting of 'character studies'.

Compare your thoughts with my suggestions about how to tackle a question which requires you to discuss or explore presentation of character. Refer to the play you are studying.

- What part does this character play in the structure of the whole play? (There is some overlap with 'role' here which we will return to.)
- In what settings do we see her or him?
- What does she/he say and do?
- What kinds of relationships does he or she have? Who are their friends, and who are their enemies?
- What do others say about them?
- What happens to them in the play as a whole?
- What appears to be the writer's attitude towards them?
- Are there any discrepancies between their speech and their actions?
- What are the distinguishing features of their speech?
- What language features do we associate with them? Think about images, symbols, particular kinds of vocabulary, for example. Remember this need not be just what they say but what the characters round about them say.
- Any movement or development in the character: do they end the play changed from how they started?
- Are we required as an audience to judge or evaluate this character?
- Do we associate this character with any significant ideas or issues in the play?
- When and why do we see him/her last? Think about what the character's fate is in the play.

Now take some time to make notes about the presentation of character in a Shakespeare play you are studying. You should find that this exercise sharpens up your responses and makes you more confident of expressing your own view, since you will have ample evidence with which to support it.

Practice and consolidation

In order to consolidate these ideas, and to link back to the issues of the preceding chapter, look closely at the following speech from *The Winter's Tale* (III, ii). You might like to keep in mind the questions based on the opening scene of this play in the last chapter (page 17).

Here Leontes's wife, Hermione, has been put on trial since her husband, suffering from irrational jealousy, is wrongly convinced that she has had an affair with his childhood friend Polixenes. Hermione has recently given birth in prison to a daughter whom her husband thinks is the child of Polixenes, not himself. This speech is given at her public trial.

HERMIONE Since what I am to say must be but that
Which contradicts my accusation, and
The testimony on my part no other
But what comes from myself, it shall scarce boot me
To say 'Not guilty': mine integrity
Being counted falsehood, shall, as I express it,
Be so received. But thus: if powers divine
Behold our human actions – as they do –
I doubt not then but innocence shall make
False accusation blush, and tyranny
Tremble at patience. You, my lord, best know –
Who least will seem to do so – my past life

Note the pause.

> Hath been as continent, as chaste, as *true*,
> As I am now unhappy; which is more
> Than history can pattern, though devised
> And played to take spectators. For behold me,
> A fellow of the royal bed, which owe
> A moiety of the throne, a great king's daughter,
> The mother to a hopeful prince, here standing
> To prate and talk for life and honour 'fore
> Who please to come and hear. For life. I prize it
> As I weigh grief, which I would spare; for honour,
> 'Tis a derivative from me to mine,
> And only that I stand for. *I appeal*
> *To your own conscience, sir, before Polixenes*
> *Came to your court,* how I was in your grace,
> How merited to be so; since he came,
> With what encounter so uncurrent I
> Have strained t'appear thus: if one jot beyond
> The bound of honour, or in act or will
> That way inclining, hardened be the hearts
> Of all that hear me, and my near'st of kin
> Cry fie upon my grave!

Commentary

The situation here is that Hermione is defending herself against a very serious accusation. Literally, her life is at stake. Let's look at the way the metre works here. Very few lines are end-stopped, and some statements extend over several lines. The units of **metre** and **syntax** do not coincide. That is, the **rhythm** of the speech does not work with the meaning of it, in one sense, in that each line is not a self-contained statement. The illusion is of natural speech, although the speech is based on **blank verse** (unrhymed 5 stress feet). The blank verse is used so flexibly that we are drawn into Hermione's world, and her desperate plight.

Notice the way in which the **choice of language** affects the audience. The word 'honour' is repeated. Hermione does not just refer to her own honour, but that of her family:

> for honour,
> 'Tis a derivative from me to mine,
> And only that I stand for.

Yet she also uses the word 'prate', in sharp contrast to the more abstract word and concept of honour, reminding us that her words count for very little in this situation.

The images she uses are not unusual in the **context** of the time. When she says 'than history can pattern, though devised/And played to take spectators', she is alluding to a common idea, that of life and drama being interlinked. History takes events and 'patterns' them, and playwrights use these events and turn them into plays which are watched by 'spectators'. This serves also to remind the audience that she is on public trial in spite of her royal birth and marriage. It is also clear that Leontes is being reminded of the enormity of what he is doing.

She also uses **personification**:

> but innocence shall make
> False accusation blush, and tyranny
> Tremble at patience.

Again, this is not an unusual feature of language in the **context** of the age. But the use of it here adds weight to her speech. The gods will be aware of her plight, and of the injustice of her husband's actions. Personifying can universalise feelings. The word 'tyranny' is striking in the **context** of the whole play, since it is an accusation that Leontes angrily denies.

On the other hand, direct addresses to her husband personalise the situation, so that he is reminded of who she is, her status, and their previous relationship.

> I appeal
> To your own conscience, sir, before Polixenes
> Came to your court,
>
> You, my lord, best know –
> Who least will seem to do so – my past life
> Hath been as continent, as chaste, as true,
> As I am now unhappy;

In this last quoted line, you should notice the way in which the word 'unhappy' occurs, not at the end of a line, but at the end of a unit of syntactical sense. It gives a pause in both the line and the meaning. We call a pause in the middle of a line of verse a **caesura**, and you should be able to observe and comment on its effects. Here there is considerable stress on the word 'unhappy' because of the rhythm of the line, and this serves to focus the audience's attention on Hermione, and to provoke their sympathy for her.

Here are the words that have been highlighted in this discussion which has been concerned not just with the **content** of the speech, but its **form and structure**. Remember the need at all times in your exam or coursework for appropriate and accurate terminology.

KEY CONCEPTS

blank verse	caesura	choice of language	context
metre	personification	rhythm	syntax

We will look further at the important idea of context later in the chapter.

2.3 Role

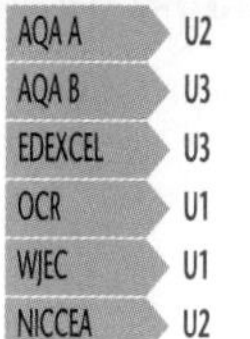

Let's move on to **role**. There is clearly much overlap between the two terms, role and **presentation**, but when you consider 'role' you need to be very clear about what a particular character contributes to the whole play. You will certainly have to bear in mind what they do and what they say. It would be useful for you to focus on their **structural contribution**, but you might also consider their **thematic significance**. You are reusing the points of presentation to an extent, but your focus now is on the pattern of the whole play.

One way of working out the role of a character is to consider what difference would be made to the play if that character did not exist. The leading characters are obviously indispensable – we couldn't have a *Macbeth* without Macbeth, clearly, so you might be asked to think about the role of less obviously important characters.

Progress check

Here are some points you could think about when considering role. Refer to the play you are studying and answer these questions.

- What scenes does this character appear in?
- Who do we usually see them with?
- What do they know?
- What do they not know?
- Do we associate them with key ideas in the play?
- What is the writer's attitude towards them?
- What is your attitude towards them?
- Is the plot changed by them?
- Are other characters changed by them?
- What difference would there be in the play as a whole without them?
- How or what do they contribute to the mood of the play?
- How do they interact with other characters?
- Do they deserve what happens to them?
- Could the play still exist without them?

What you are looking at here could be put in another way. Think about the contribution the character makes in terms of the following:

- Plot
- Ideas
- Patterns
- Dramatic impact
- Contrast
- Parallels
- Structure
- Mood

2.4 Relationships

AQA A	U2
AQA B	U3
EDEXCEL	U3
OCR	U1
WJEC	U1
NICCEA	U2

Let's think now about **relationships** and their presentation in Shakespeare's plays.

Take a few moments to write down points about what seems to you to be a significant relationship in a play you are studying. Note down who the characters are in the relationship, and what it is that seems to you to be significant.

Progress check

These are all key questions. The last two are increasingly important in recent critical approaches to Shakespeare and other writers of his age. Critics are debating issues about the relationships between literary texts and 'history', pointing out the difficulty of differentiating between these two concepts. Refer to the play you are studying and answer these questions.

Here are some points that seem to me to be worth noting about relationships in the plays.

- Who is the dominating partner?
- What does each gain from the relationship?
- What brings people together?
- How do they affect one another?
- Does each partner change?
- Are relationships between men and women similar to those between men and men, and women and women?
- Can there really be true equality in a relationship?
- What does the relationship contribute to your understanding of the ideas in the whole play?
- What part does it play in the plot and structure of the play?
- What language is used to describe it?
- How does each partner speak?
- How does the audience find out what each partner feels about the other?
- Is love a more powerful emotion than hatred?
- Is Shakespeare more interested in friendship or sexual love?
- Which is more important in the plays?
- How important are feelings generally?
- Are they primary or secondary in the plays as a whole?
- Is it possible for us to understand or even empathise with characters in plays written 400 or so years ago?
- Does it make sense even to try?

ASSESSMENT OBJECTIVES

AO5i: Literary texts do themselves form history, and in order to make sense of past events, we tell ourselves stories, make up narratives about them. Modern critics would no longer accept that we can step back from a period and survey it in a detached and unprejudiced way. We are bound to bring our own prejudices and preconceptions to bear even if we aren't aware of it and don't acknowledge it. Tillyard's 'Elizabethan world picture' is a case in point. You may well have come across his ideas about the way that people in Elizabethan times thought and conceptualised. We have to treat this with extreme caution, realising that Tillyard had his own agenda, with a very particular picture of the England of his time – facing war – influencing his interpretation. In any case, he greatly simplified a much more complex picture.
If you are interested in these ideas, you will find that **New Historicist** and **Cultural Materialist** critics are the ones to read up on since they look at the importance of all kinds of issues concerning history and context.
These ideas and issues are all relevant to the concept of context which is now very important in A Level studies in English Literature.

If we return now to the topic of relationships, it's worth pointing out that in spite of the need for caution about any assumptions we may be inclined to make about the motives and feelings of the people of Shakespeare's time, let alone the dramatic conventions of his day, you can still learn a great deal about the plays by a consideration of relationships in them.

For one thing, you will be focused on the issue of **power**. We have already discussed this in relation to Perdita and Florizel in the extract from *The Winter's Tale* quoted and discussed in the last chapter. What we did there was to attempt to identify the underlying power relations. This also is a really important aspect of New Historicism. Who really has a choice in the plays? Does Shakespeare allow the less powerful to have a say, or do the powerful ultimately call all the shots?

Progress check

Think about the issue of power in a play you are studying. Take a few minutes to identify the real sources of power in the plays, and try to decide what view the play as a whole endorses. This last point is crucial.

- When the play has ended what are we left with?
- Has the social order been restored?
- Has there been a change of power?

One thing you may find is that some characters have relatively little choice. In *The Winter's Tale*, for example, Leontes, King of Sicilia, instructs Camillo (whom we met in the first scene) to kill Polixenes, King of Bohemia, in the mistaken belief that his old friend has made Leontes's wife, Hermione, pregnant. What choice does Camillo have? As you would expect, very little. He is forced to leave his country and go into enforced exile, working for Polixenes. This exile lasts for 16 years. It is only by a series of strange and fateful events, along with his own cleverness and resourcefulness, that he is able to return to Sicilia. In fact, Leontes's irrational behaviour brings about many unfortunate and even tragic outcomes for others. His position of power means that no one can effectively oppose him. Things are eventually put right more or less, but there is a great deal of suffering before this happens. Leontes participates in that suffering and comes to realise the consequences of his own actions, but other characters in the play do not have that choice. And although the play offers criticism of his 'tyranny', largely through female characters, still we have to wait for the king's change of heart. Patience and suffering may be part of Leontes's redemption, but they are enforced and involuntary for the lesser characters.

AO4: One of the things that will be pointed out by **feminist** critics is the lack of power and choice of female characters in the plays.

Progress check

Write down the names of two or three female characters in the play or plays you are studying. Follow this by quick notes on their power or lack of it.

Commentary

This is an interesting question because it does raise obvious difficulties for a modern audience. If we leave aside *The Taming of the Shrew* with its seemingly misogynist subject matter, we still have fertile ground for discussion and debate.

Even the most spirited, intelligent and accomplished of Shakespeare's heroines seem to offer us mixed messages. There's the disguise as men, for example. Portia from *The Merchant of Venice* shows us what women are capable of, but only in the guise of men. Otherwise, she has to act according to the will of men. This is literally so in the case of her dead father's will which she must obey. In spite of her grumbles to Nerissa, her maid, she does not seriously object to carrying out his will. She is also willing to hand over all that is hers to her new husband, Bassanio. It is hard for a modern-day audience not to feel that the winner in this deal is Bassanio, not Portia. She seems to bring a great deal more in every way than he does. In the end, though, the play endorses the will of the men, apparently. The male decision is the right decision. The play as a whole avoids conflict since Portia's choice coincides with that produced by her father's will. Portia may outwit Bassanio in some ways, but she has handed over such power that she has without a second thought.

Of course, the fact that female characters were played by boys must have affected both the way these roles were created and shaped and the way they were played. **Ambiguity** is increased when the woman who is already a boy dresses as a boy.

You may have noticed in your plays references to the nature of women. We cannot take these as Shakespeare's own views as they always have a **context**. Hamlet's 'Frailty, thy name is woman' has to be seen as part of his own tortured state of mind and is rather showing us his feelings about his mother's actions. But other characters tend to generalise about women's actions, morals and weaknesses in the plays. In *The Winter's Tale*, both the kings, Leontes and Polixenes, make assumptions about women: they stereotype them. Leontes sees all women as betrayers, liars and adulterers. Because he has falsely accused his wife of adultery, he extends this accusation to all women. If they are not young and attractive as he sees it, then he imposes another stereotype – the scold, the hen-pecking wife. Polixenes thinks his son, Florizel, can only have fallen in love with Perdita, apparently a shepherd's daughter, because she has 'bewitched' him.

> And thou, fresh piece
> Of excellent witchcraft, who of force must know
> The royal fool thou cop'st with.

If you examine Polixenes's assumptions here, you can see that he takes it for granted that his son, 'the royal fool', has been manipulated by Perdita who cannot possibly be innocent. Yet if you remember the extract from the play given in the last chapter, you will realise that Perdita is much more hesitant and apprehensive than Florizel who has all the confidence of power and rank.

In *Othello* Iago finds it easy in the end to persuade Othello that Desdemona could not have loved him, that she is promiscuous, that Othello got his signals mixed: he misunderstood her sophistication. Iago says:

> I know our country disposition well.
> In Venice they do let God see the pranks
> They dare not show their husbands; their best conscience
> Is not to leave't undone, but keep it unknown

Here, Iago generalises about city women like Desdemona, implying that Othello is just too naive to understand what the married women of Venice are really like. He is playing on Othello's insecurities.

In fact, there are several outsiders in Shakespeare's plays, like Othello, or Shylock. Or characters like Hamlet who in a sense choose the role of outsider rather than having it given to them because of race or colour. Because plays are based on conflict, unequal distribution of power matters, and that is one reason why women could also be said to be outsiders since they almost always lack power and authority in Shakespeare's world.

We are clearly not meant to respond by agreeing with Iago's view here. We have evidence for ourselves that Desdemona loves Othello. We can see the great insecurity in the man which leaves him vulnerable to Iago's suggestions of naïvety, in the matters of love. Yet the play *Othello* as a whole offers us a curious view of women where we have three apparent types: the pure Desdemona, the down-to-earth and coarser Emilia, and the prostitute Bianca. To make your mind up on this issue, you will need to consider the whole play. What view of women does the play endorse? The tragedies can seem so much men's tragedies, as if the female characters are lesser, so that their fate (which can be death too in the plays: think about Desdemona and Emilia in *Othello*, Gertrude and Ophelia in *Hamlet*) is somehow of less significance than that of the men.

Another aspect to think about is the way in which we see female characters through male eyes, and that they move in a masculine world. This is true of the characters in the plays in two senses: they are seen through the eyes of male characters, and judged by them, but they are also created by male writers, and played by male actors. So if these female characters, such as Portia, are often seen as 'strong', whose criteria are we using? Perhaps they are 'strong' only in what has traditionally been seen as a masculine way.

It is worth thinking about this interesting approach to the plays, which again is very much part of current critical thinking.

KEY CONCEPTS

ambiguity	context	Cultural Materialist
feminist	New Historicist	power

2.5 Ways into your Shakespeare play

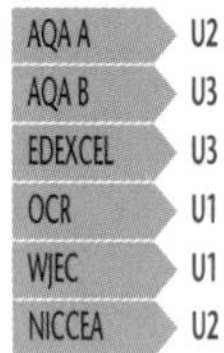

Here are some ways in which you can examine the play or plays you are studying. In this way you are making your own independent judgements, whilst still paying close attention to the details of the play and the fact that it is meant to be performed and not simply read and studied.

This is a series of comments about *Othello* – agree or disagree with the following statements:

- It is crucial to the play that Othello is an outsider.
- Desdemona is too naïve – she brings her fate on herself.
- 'One who loved not wisely, but too well' is a good summing up of Othello's behaviour.
- Iago is presented to us as a more interesting character than Othello.
- Justice is done at the end of the play.
- Sexual jealousy is the most important issue in the play.
- Emilia plays a crucial role in the play.
- The tragedy is as much Desdemona's as Othello's.

Progress check

You can apply this idea to a text you are studying. Having to agree or disagree is what makes this a useful exercise. If you work with someone else, you can prepare a series of statements each.

The following statements can be applied to any play:

- Pick out five key words from or about the play: these could be words frequently repeated, used only once or twice but with great significance, or words which sum up important ideas or issues in the play.
- What is the turning point of the play? You could identify any part of the play (up to 50/60 lines).
- Find three significant links or parallels in the play: you could look for words or phrases which are repeated in different contexts, situations which re-occur, or parallel relationships, for example.
- Find two examples of foreshadowing.
- What is the most dramatic moment of the play?
- Choose three speeches by a leading character, from different stages of the play, which demonstrate their varying states of mind. Explain why you've chosen them.

> These are all questions which should help you to **analyse** and understand any dramatic text. You will be on the way to meeting all the assessment objectives, but in particular, AO3: **show understanding of the ways in which writers' choices of form, structure and language shape meanings;** and AO4: **articulate independent opinions and judgements, informed by different interpretations of literary texts by other readers.** In order for you to prepare the way for the exploration of others' judgements, you will need to clarify and justify your own, by detailed reference to the text.
>
> ASSESSMENT OBJECTIVES

2.6 Different interpretations

AQA A	U2
AQA B	U3
EDEXCEL	U3
OCR	U1
WJEC	U1
NICCEA	U2

You will need to be aware of the idea of multiple interpretations. There is no one way of reading a text, and much of what is read depends on the reader and their situation. As we have already seen, this has another dimension in drama, since individual performances are also interpretations. There is no such thing as a definitive performance for everyone, or one final reading of any text. In the process of reading critics, or listening to others' views about the play, you will be able to form your own independent judgement. And you will be meeting AO5i (which requires you to show understanding of the contexts in which literary texts are written and **understood**) as well as the other objectives, including AO4 (which requires you to articulate independent opinions and judgements, informed by different interpretations by other readers).

Look, for example, at some critics' comments on *Othello*. You will see a variety of responses depending on the period of writer, and their gender and attitude to literature.

> Othello is incapable of learning from experience. (F.R. Leavis, 1937)
>
> The tragedy of Othello develops because Othello is drawn into Iago's view of the world. (Jan Kott, 1967)
>
> The audience is 'expected to feel a good deal of sympathy' for Iago's 'thwarted sense of superiority'. (William Empson, 1977)
>
> Othello is even more tragic, because the suffering could so easily have been avoided. (David Margolies, 1992)
>
> [Act IV, scene iii:] In this scene, Desdemona represents female passivity. Emilia is more assertive, and the scene shows the struggle between male and female responsibility. (Lisa Jardine, 1994)
>
> This scene shows us that Othello's jealousy is linked to possession, and challenges the male view of events. It shows the play is 'a specifically masculine tragedy'. (Kiernan Ryan, 1995)

It is not possible to find one **correct** reading of a play, or any piece of literature. What we can do is be aware of our own ideas and preconceptions, as well as being alert to those of others. And of course we have to be able to find the textual evidence to support our ideas.

2.7 Text, context and meaning

AQA A	U2
AQA B	U3
EDEXCEL	U3
OCR	U1
WJEC	U1
NICCEA	U2

The idea of context has been referred to throughout this chapter. This is because it is an important idea in the new AS and A level specifications. Not everyone feels comfortable with this idea, but it is important that you get to grips with it.

The Assessment Objective which is crucial here is AO5(i): **show understanding of the contexts in which literary texts are written and understood.**

When you come to the A2 year, this objective is developed with AO5(ii): **evaluate the significance of cultural, historical and other contextual influences on literary texts and study.**

In order to assess what you already know about context (even though you may think this is very little!) think about the following statements, and decide whether you agree or disagree with them.

In order to fully understand a text it is necessary to:

- know something about the author and their life
- understand the historical period in which the text was written and/or published
- have some kind of understanding of the author's beliefs and attitudes
- read widely in order to find out what other critics and readers have thought about the text
- understand the influence of the author's gender on their work
- consider the influence of the author's race on their work
- understand the technical features of the work
- know something about the genre of the work
- understand how this text has been influenced by earlier ones
- none of these – a text should stand by itself without having to refer to any other material.

It used to be thought that the final statement was the only way of approaching literature. The New Critics of England and America, in the 1930s and 1940s, believed that there was no need for any other kind of knowledge than the text itself. Yet although this may sound sensible, think about how much knowledge you already apply when you read texts.

For example, you might already be aware of the conditions of the theatre of Shakespeare's time. You will certainly need to know about the conventions of the **genre**. You will not read a play in the same way as a novel, because a play is meant to be performed, and you need to be aware of the **stage conventions** of his time and ours. As you will have already studied **other** plays by Shakespeare, you will, I am sure, apply what you already know from this study to the reading of a new play. You may well also be aware of some of the ideas and conditions of Shakespeare's **time**, and if you know anything about his **life** you probably think it is relevant to a study of his plays.

Applying context

If you look at the categories above, you will find suggestions that will help you to think about the importance of context.

In order to apply these ideas, we will look briefly at the play *Antony and Cleopatra*. AO5 refers to the ways in which texts 'are written and understood'. It is quite closely linked with AO4 which requires you to demonstrate your own 'judgements', informed by 'different interpretations of literary texts by other readers'. You can see how these two AOs are linked in the way in which different judgements are formed about texts depending on who is judging and the context in which the judgement is being made.

The play *Antony and Cleopatra* tells the story of two great leaders, Antony, the Roman, and Cleopatra, Queen of Egypt, their love affair and their ultimate downfall. Politics and personal life are mixed, and Shakespeare explores the clashing of different values and ways of life.

It is a play very much dependent on opinions: characters feel free to comment on the two protagonists and their behaviour, usually with disapproval. In fact, the play actually begins with two Romans criticising Antony for his reckless and, as they see it, irresponsible behaviour, and Cleopatra who is described as a kind of prostitute. Antony is judged as besotted with Cleopatra, and in that way much weakened and a lesser man than he used to be.

Many earlier critics have seen Antony as the hero of the play and have been less than complimentary about Cleopatra. William Hazlitt in *A View of the English Stage* [1813] said: Cleopatra is " voluptuous, ostentatious, conscious, boastful of her charms, haughty, tyrannical, fickle..

A W *Schlegel Lectures on Dramatic Literature* [1840] wrote that 'Cleopatra is as remarkable for her seductive charms as Antony for the splendour of his deeds.'

Edward Dowden in Shakespeare : A Critical Study of His Mind and Art [1875] argued: 'At every moment we are necessarily aware of the gross, the mean, the disorderly womanhood in Cleopatra, no less than of the witchery and wonder which excite, and charm, and subdue. We see her a dissembler, a termagant, a coward; and yet "vilest things become her". The presence of a spirit of life quick, shifting, multitudinous, incalculable, fascinates the eye, and would, if it could, lull the moral sense to sleep.'

You can see the trend of these comments which is to place the majority of the blame on Cleopatra who is seen as immoral and manipulative. The tendency is to judge her as the woman who leads a great man astray. Her own political role is downplayed or ignored altogether.

Some twentieth century critics have seen Cleopatra as embodying eternal woman.

Harley Granville-Barker in Prefaces to Shakespeare [1930] equates this with the state of being a child: 'The passionate woman has a child's desires and a child's fears, an animal's wary distrust; balance of judgement none, one would say. But often, she shows the shrewd scepticism of a child.'

S L Bethell in *Shakespeare and the Popular Dramatic Tradition* [1944] argued that Shakespeare 'in Cleopatra presents the mystery of woman.'

Daniel Stempel in *The Transmigration of the Crocodile* [1956] relates these ideas more to context, though perhaps unaware of the prejudice behind his own comments: 'Here our knowledge of Elizabethan mores can come to our aid. Woman was a creature of weak reason and strong passion, carnal in nature and governed by lust. She could be trusted only when guided by the wisdom of her natural superior, man...The misogyny of Octavius Caesar is founded on right reason.'

Look at the following critical views, quite closely related in period:

Derek Traversi: *Shakespeare: The Roman Plays* [1963]. 'The student of Antony and Cleopatra has, in offering an account of this great tragedy, to resolve the problem of approach, of the author's intention. Sooner or later, he finds himself faced by two possible readings of the play, whose only difficulty is that they seem to be mutually exclusive.'

A P Riemer in A Reading of *Shakespeare's Antony and Cleopatra* [1968]. '*Antony and Cleopatra* can be read as the fall of a great general, betrayed in his dotage by a treacherous strumpet, or else it can be viewed as a celebration of transcendental love.'

How do you respond to those two opinions? You perhaps noted that the 'student' in Traversi's comment is male. Characteristic of its time, in which 'he' was argued to include 'she', yet might this not influence the view stated? The assumption is made here that the meaning of the play resides in the writer's 'intention' rather than in the varying responses to the play through time. Look at the language used by Riemer to describe Cleopatra, and the way in which Antony's status is identified whilst hers is ignored. The alternative to the crude judgement on Antony and Cleopatra, which Reimer is, of course, not necessarily endorsing, is the 'transcendental love'. The play is by and large taken away from its politics and personalised.

LT Fitz responds to these sorts of opinions in Egyptian Queens and Male Reviewers: Sexist Attitudes in Antony and Cleopatra Criticism [1977]. She argues that the reduction of the play's action to ' the fall of a great general ' and the definition of the play's major interest as ' transcendental love' make a reasonable assessment of the character of Cleopatra impossible.

Fitz, an early feminist critic, explores an alternative view of Cleopatra and provides a reading of Cleopatra that called for a re-centring of the interests of the play. Different judgements are applied to these tow leading characters. Cleopatra has been criticised for trying to save her own political skin after the battle of Actium when she makes some political approaches to Caesar - whereas when Antony leaves Egypt and marries Octavia, Caesar's sister, in a political move designed to please Caesar he is praised. It has been claimed that Antony is the protagonist - yet he dies in Act IV. Fitz argues that the play culminates in Cleopatra's death scene; she has more speeches than Antony but her speeches contain fewer lines than Antony's and that she grows as Antony does not.

Fitz takes issus with A C Bradley (a critic writing 100 years ago yet still frequently used by today's exam candidates) declares that the play is not a true tragedy because he cannot find the tragic hero's inner struggle in Antony. But Cleopatra has that inner struggle. It is the fact that she is female that has caused her to be sidelined by such critics who see 'greatness' as being a male characteristic, but who are unaware of their own biased judgements.

Kenneth Parker in *Antony and Cleopatra*: Writers and their Works [2000] sums up by arguing that probably no other female figure in a Shakespeare play is criticised to the extent that Cleopatra is. She is abused with a variety of ways which, no matter how poetically these are sometimes expressed, in the end, nevertheless, come down to one simple assertion: that the Queen of Egypt is a whore!

This is an example of the kinds of comments which have been made over almost 200 years about one of Shakespeare's plays. You can see in them the changes that have occurred in range and emphasis. These changes are, of course, related to the times in which they were written and attitudes that were prevalent, as well as unspoken assumptions about, for example the role of men and women, politically and personally.

Sample question and model answer

Practice and consolidation: Othello

What does this dialogue show us about the interactions of these characters? You should refer closely to the language to support your answer.

Desdemona, daughter of Brabantio, has secretly married Othello, a black general older than her, and much honoured by the Venetian state. Iago, Othello's 'ancient', a kind of regimental sergeant-major equivalent, is secretly making trouble for Othello, rousing Brabantio with insulting references to Othello's colour. Othello is sought by the state, in the person of the Duke, to help the fight in Cyprus against the enemy, the Turks. Othello has just explained how he wooed Desdemona by telling her about his adventures in battle.

This extract is taken from Act I, scene iii

DUKE The Turk with a most mighty preparation makes for Cyprus. Othello, the fortitude of the place is best known to you. And though we have there a substitute of most allowed sufficiency; yet opinion, a more sovereign mistress of effects throws a more safer voice on you. You must therefore be content to slubber the gloss of your new fortunes, with this more stubborn, and boisterous expedition.

Note change from prose to verse. Change of tone, subject?

OTHELLO The Tyrant Custom, most grave Senators,
Hath made the flinty and steel couch of War
My thrice-driven bed of down. I do agonize
A natural and prompt alacrity,
I find in hardness: and do undertake
This present wars against the Ottomites.
Most humbly therefore bending to your State,
I crave fit disposition for my wife,
Due reference of place, and exhibition,
With such accommodation and besort
As levels with her breeding.

Look at pace, rhythm, here.

DUKE Why, at her father's.

BRABANTIO (I will not have it so.)

OTHELLO (Nor I.)

DESDEMONA Nor would I there reside
To put my father in impatient thoughts
By being in his eye. Most gracious Duke,
To my unfolding, lend your prosperous ear,
And let me find a charter in your voice
T'assist my simpleness.

DUKE What would you Desdemona?

DESDEMONA That I did love the Moor, to live with him
My downright violence, and storm of fortunes,
May trumpet to the world. My heart's subdu'd
Even to that very quality of my lord.
I saw Othello's visage in his mind,
And to his honours and his valiant parts
Did I my soul and fortunes consecrate.
So that (dear lords) if I be left behind

Image - what does it convey?

A moth of peace, and he go to the war,
The rites for why I love him, are bereft me:
And I a heavy interim shall support
By his dear absence. Let me go with him.

OTHELLO Let her have your voice.
Vouch with me Heaven, I therefore beg it not
To please the palate of my appetite:
Nor to comply with heat the young affects
In me defunct, and proper satisfaction.

Sample question and model answer (continued)

Look how seriously Othello takes his post. He will not be distracted.

Look at rhythm of these lines.

Opposition.

Foreshadowing.

But to be free and bounteous to her mind:
And Heaven defend your good souls, that you think
I will your serious and great business scant
When she is with me. No, when light-wing'd toys
Of feather'd Cupid, seel with wanton dullness
My speculative, and offic'd instrument:
That my disports corrupt, and taint my business:
Let housewives make a skillet of my helm,
And all indign, and base adversities,
Make head against my estimation.

DUKE Be it as you shall privately determine,
Either for her stay, or going: th'affair cries haste:
And speed must answer it.

SENATOR You must away tonight.

DESDEMONA Tonight, my lord?

DUKE (This night.)

OTHELLO (With all my heart.)

DUKE At nine in th'morning here we'll meet again.
Othello, leave some officer behind,
And he shall our commission bring to you:
And such things else of quality and respect
As doth import you.

OTHELLO So please your Grace, my Ancient,
A man he is of honesty and trust:
to his conveyance I assign my wife,
With what else needful, your good Grace shall think
To be sent after me.

DUKE (Let it be so:)
Good night to every one. And noble Signor,
If virtue no delighted beauty lack,
Your son-in-law is far more fair than black.

SENATOR Adieu brave Moor, use Desdemona well.

BRABANTIO **Look to her Moor, if thou hast eyes to see.**
She has deceiv'd her father, and may thee.

Exeunt Duke, Senators, Officers

Commentary

We see here the interaction between characters, but more than this, between public and private lives, domesticity and the state, peace and war, occupation and love. These **oppositions** form part of the **pattern** of the play. Desdemona has had to make a choice between her father and her husband, and now she asserts herself in requesting that she be allowed to accompany her husband to war. We are aware that she has put herself into a vulnerable situation, as we see that her father no longer wishes to have anything to do with her. This vulnerability emphasises the lack of **power** of women at that time, and the extent to which they are dependent on men.

Othello is clearly a man of reputation and ability, as the Duke's words make plain. There is a sense of urgency in the **rhythm** of the lines:

SENATOR You must away tonight
DESDEMONA (Tonight, my lord?)
DUKE (This night.)
OTHELLO (With all my heart.)

Sample question and model answer (continued)

Look at the ways in which the speakers complete each other's lines **metrically**. It would be useful to compare this to the scene from *Hamlet* discussed in the previous chapter.

And it is also clear that Othello has a great pride in his own abilities as a soldier. He does not want to be seen as taking his wife with him in order to neglect his duties as a general. The love between Othello and Desdemona is openly declared but he also declares his determination not to be distracted from his work on the island.

> And Heaven defend your good souls, that you think
> I will your serious and great business scant
> When she is with me.

Othello believes in the seriousness of his tasks and duties, much as he loves Desdemona. The Duke is concerned to reassure Brabantio, but the terms in which he addresses him betray his attitudes as what we now in our **context** would call racist:

> And noble Signor,
> If virtue no delighted beauty lack,
> Your son-in-law is far more fair than black.

The Duke sets up another **opposition** in the play, that of black and white, but fairness is associated with virtue. Yet the **rhyming couplet** inevitably makes the sentiment expressed by the Duke seem trite and trivial.

The last words spoken by Brabantio are an example of **foreshadowing**. They seem to be of great importance, though at this stage the audience will not be fully aware of their real significance. However, later the words return to haunt Othello, as he is persuaded by Iago that Desdemona is unfaithful. And it is worth pointing out that no audience is going to be unaware of the plot of the play. It is quite likely that most modern audiences will be familiar with the text, or even studying it. Therefore, to such an audience, foreshadowing brings with it a recognition of the full significance of the words. The trust in Iago displayed by Othello is also significant as the audience is already aware of the malice that Iago has towards Othello. This is a point always worth knowing when you are considering drama: what knowledge does the audience have? Usually the audience is in a privileged position, with insight into events that the characters on stage do not have.

KEY CONCEPTS

dramatic interaction	foreshadowing	gender
issues and ideas	mood	oppositions
patterns	power	rhyming couplet
rhythm and metre	values	

Sample question and model answer (continued)

Comparison of student answers

Compare the openings of two student answers. Which is better and why?

The question is based on an extract from *Henry V* (set by Edexcel). The scene (from Act IV, scene i) is set the night before the battle of Agincourt, and the king moves around the camp in disguise listening to the views of the ordinary soldiers, of whom Williams is a representative figure.

> WILLIAMS But if the cause be not good, the king himself hath a heavy reckoning to make; when all those legs and arms and heads, chopped off in a battle, shall join together at the latter day, and cry all, 'We died at such a place'; some swearing, some crying for a surgeon, some upon their wives left poor behind them, some upon the debts they owe, some upon their children rawly left. I am afeard there are few that die well that die in a battle; for how can they charitably dispose of any thing when blood is their argument? Now, if these men do not die well, it will be a black matter for the king that led them to it, who to disobey were against all proportion of subjection.
>
> KING HENRY So, if a son that is by his father sent about merchandise do sinfully miscarry upon the sea, the imputation of his wickedness, by your rule, should be imposed upon his father that sent him: or if a servant, under his master's command transporting a sum of money, be assailed by robbers and die in many irreconciled iniquities, you may call the business of the master the author of the servant's damnation. But this is not so: the king is not bound to answer the particular endings of his soldiers, the father of his son, nor the master his servant; for they purpose not their death when they purpose their services.

How does Shakespeare dramatically present the argument between Williams and the king? Which of them is meant to gain the audience's sympathy?

Answer A

'Their children rawly left'. Williams uses an image which vividly evokes pain and terror, and which shows the audience that he has real experience of war, and that war has real effects on ordinary people, including those left bereaved at home. The word 'rawly' suggests pain and vulnerability. In contrast the king argues logically. He presents a rational argument based on authority figures, and his language, in contrast to Williams', is dry, legalistic and spare. He seems to deny the 'heavy reckoning' that Williams believes is due to a king who leads men to die horribly in battle that cannot be fully justified.

Answer B

In this extract, the king and Williams show a lot of differences in their attitudes to war. They discuss who is responsible for the deaths that happen. Williams thinks that kings should take responsibility for the deaths, but the king argues that he is no more responsible than a father whose son dies undertaking a task on his behalf, or a master for the death of a servant.

Commentary

Both these students are writing under exam conditions, which means that they have to say all that they can within a limited time.

- Which of them gets to the point most quickly?

  A obviously approaches the text immediately.
  B writes at a distance from the text.

Sample question and model answer *(continued)*

- Which of them analyses?

  A seizes hold of the issues and language straightaway,
  B explains what is happening.

- Which of them argues?

  There is an immediate sense of an argument in A,
  but none noticeably yet in B.

- Which of them shows a grasp of dramatic techniques and effects?

  A contrasts the language of the two speakers, starting an argument we feel will be later developed.
  B shows no awareness that this is a play.

- Which of them uses appropriate terminology?

  The vocabulary in A is accurate, and introduces the idea of images and their effects. The words which explain and analyse the effects of the contrasting dialogue are precise and thoughtful.

  The language of B shows no familiarity with literary terminology.

Although we were looking only at the openings of answers the qualities of each response were evident. You need to make your introductions work for you, in order to convince your examiner that you can analyse and argue, based on strong textual evidence, and with an awareness of genre.

LEARNING SUMMARY

The ideas and skills that have been discussed in this chapter are relevant to both exams and coursework. As well as an analysis of dramatic techniques, with practical examples, we have also considered the importance of assessment objectives, how to tackle an exam question, and how to demonstrate to examiners the skills and knowledge that are being tested. In particular we have looked at AOs 3, 4 and 5, considering the ways in which they are interlinked. We have examined the ways in which you can make use of critics and reviewers in forming your own judgements, and the importance of a focus on genre.

We considered the presentation of character, relationships and role, as well as the significance of issues of power and the lack of it in the plays.

Exam practice and analysis

Here is a possible coursework task

How does Shakespeare present relationships between men and women in *Much Ado about Nothing*, and how might a modern audience respond to them?

AOs targeted: AO5i (double-weighted), AO1, AO2i, AO3, AO4

Notes

Context [AO5i] is addressed in the reference to the differences between the attitudes and assumptions implicit in the text and shown through 'presentation' and a possible modern response.

The word 'audience' draws attention to the genre of the text [AO2i], reminding you that the play is meant to be performed, not just read.

The words 'how does' and 'presents' focus on AO3, and you should examine and explore Shakespeare's techniques, not merely write about what happens in the play.

You need to demonstrate, with appropriate textual evidence, your own argument, showing that you can form an opibion which is your own, even if you refer to other critics. [AO4]

The way that you use literary terminology and the fluency of your written English is the focus of the AO1 assessment.

The length of the essay varies according to the demands of the different boards – ranging from 1000 to 2000 words.

Chapter 3

Poetry

After studying this chapter you should know about:

- *place of assessment, importance of AOs*
- *form and structure*
- *patterns and sounds*
- *the significance of context*
- *the creation of a voice*
- *choice of language*
- *right and wrong way to answer a question*

LEARNING OBJECTIVES

3.1 Assessment

AQA A	U3
AQA B	U2
EDEXCEL	U1
OCR	U2
WJEC	U3
NICCEA	U1

Every AS specification includes poetry, but not all boards assess it in the same way. Here is a table of the texts on the specifications of the main boards: you should look particularly at the way the assessment objectives are met.

AQA A

Texts in Context

AOs 1, 2i, 3, 4, 5i, especially 4 and 5i Open Book one hour question

Geoffrey Chaucer: *The Miller's Prologue and Tale*
Thomas Hardy: *Selected Poems*
Selected Poems of the Brontës
Philip Larkin: *High Windows*
Carol Ann Duffy: *The World's Wife*

(depending on choice of drama, might be pre-twentieth century or not)

AQA B

AOs 2i: 5%; 3: and 10% Closed Text

one hour question as part of poetry and drama exam

Geoffrey Chaucer: *The Miller's Tale*
John Donne: *Selected Poems*
John Milton: *Paradise Lost,* Book 1
William Blake: *Songs of Innocence and Experience*
A.E. Housman: *A Shropshire Lad*
John Keats: *Selected Poems*

NICCEA

AOs 2i: 10%; 3: 10%; 4: 10%; 5: 10% Open Book

Emily Dickinson: *Selected Poems*
Seamus Heaney: *Opened Ground*
Gerard Manley Hopkins: *Selected Poems*
Edward Thomas: *Selected Poems*
Stevie Smith: *Selected Poems*
W.B. Yeats: *Selected Poems*

EDEXCEL

Open Book 1 hour (AOs 1, 2i, 3, 4, equally divided)

Gillian Clarke: *Letter from a Far Country*
John Betjeman: *Best of Betjeman*
John Keats: *Selected Poems*
Penguin Book of American Verse
Edexcel Anthology

OCR

Open Book

Geoffrey Chaucer: *The Franklin's Tale*
Browning: *Selected Poems*
Byron: *Selected Poems*
T.S. Eliot: *Selected Poems*
Tony Harrison: *Selected Poems*
Shakespeare: *The Complete Sonnets*
Anne Stevenson: *Granny Scarecrow*

WJEC

Twentieth century:

Carol Ann Duffy: *Selected Poems*
Seamus Heaney: *Selected Poems*
Philip Larkin: *Whitsun Weddings*
Eavan Boland: *Selected Poems*
Dannie Abse: *Welsh Retrospective*
Dylan Thomas: *Selected Poems*
W.B. Yeats: *Selected Poems*
Ted Hughes: *Selected Poems*

As you can see from this table, there is a wide variety of poetry available on the different specifications. In this chapter, we will first examine form, structure and language, focusing on individual poems, then apply these techniques to poems taken from the different specifications, from different periods. There will be a particular focus on poems which appear in more than one specification. We will also examine questions, and mark schemes, looking critically at different student responses.

ASSESSMENT OBJECTIVES

AO3: Show detailed understanding of the ways in which writers' choices of form, structure and language shape meanings.

The words 'form, structure and language' seem straightforward, but they do cause difficulty in their interpretation and application. But if you look closely at this AO, you can see that there are clues about how to understand what is meant. The words 'writers' choices', for example, are helpful. They show that you can consider the ways in which one choice would be different in its effect from another. The word 'shape' indicates that there is a crafting happening when writers write, that conscious decisions are made; but 'meanings' tells you that the meanings are not just those intended by the writer, but those which are given by individual readers in response to the writers' choices. And different readers at different times will inevitably respond in varying ways, which clearly links in to AO5i.

3.2 Form and structure

AQA A	U3
AQA B	U2
EDEXCEL	U1
OCR	U2
WJEC	U3
NICCEA	U1

The meaning of these two terms is very closely connected. It is often useful to think of a poem, or any piece of writing, in terms of its journey: where is the writer going and by what stages does she/he arrive at the destination?

This image will give you the basic idea of the structure of a poem, but think about how the writer chooses to set the poem out on the page. There is a strong focus on this in a poem, and the form of a poem will affect its meaning.

The following example is a poem by the American poet, Lawrence Ferlinghetti (born 1919). It is based on a print by Gustav Klimt, called *The Kiss*, and what you have here are the words of the poem, though not their **form** on the page.

Short Story on a Painting of Gustav Klimt

They are kneeling upright on a flowered bed He has just caught her there and holds her still Her gown has slipped down off her shoulder He has an urgent hunger His dark head bends to hers hungrily And the woman the woman turns her tangerine lips from his one hand like the head of a dead swan draped over his heavy neck the fingers strangely crimped together her other arm doubled up against her tight breast her hand a languid claw clutching his hand which would turn her mouth to his her long dress made of multicolored blossoms quilted on gold her Titian hair with blue stars in it And his gold harlequin robe checkered with dark squares Gold garlands stream down over her bare calves & tensed feet Nearby there must be a jeweled tree with glass leaves aglitter in the gold air It must be morning in a faraway place somewhere They are silent together as in a flowered field upon the summer couch which must be hers And he holds her still so passionately holds her head to his so gently so insistently to make her turn her lips to his her eyes are closed like folded petals She will not open he is not the One.

(Lawrence Ferlinghetti)

The original poem has no punctuation apart from the capital letters shown, and its meaning depends on the position of the words on the page – its **form**. There is no rhyme or regular metre to guide you here, simply the arrangement of the words to form the **shape** of the poem.

Try to arrange these words (they are in the right order, remember) into a poem. What you should be trying to do here is not to reproduce the original which would be impossible, but to turn these words into a shape that has meaning for you.

When you have done this, look at the original poem below, and compare it to your version.

Short Story on a Painting of Gustav Klimt

They are kneeling upright on a flowered bed
He
has just caught her there
and holds her still
Her gown
has slipped down
off her shoulder
He has an urgent hunger
His dark head
bends to hers
hungrily
And the woman the woman
turns her tangerine lips from his
one hand like the head of a dead swan
draped down over
his heavy neck
the fingers
strangely crimped
tightly together
her other arm doubled up
against her tight breast
her hand a languid claw
clutching his hand
which would turn her mouth
to his
her long dress made
of multicolored blossoms
quilted on gold
her Titian hair
with blue stars in it
And his gold
harlequin robe
checkered with
dark squares
Gold garlands
stream down over
her bare calves &
tensed feet
Nearby there must be
a jeweled tree
with glass leaves aglitter
in the gold air
It must be
morning
in a faraway place somewhere
They are silent together
as in a flowered field
upon the summer couch
which must be hers
And he holds her still
so passionately
holds her head to his
so gently so insistently
to make her turn
her lips to his
her eyes are closed
like folded petals
She
will not open
He
is not the One. (Lawrence Ferlinghetti)

Commentary

Here are some comments made by students who have tried this exercise. See how they compare to your ideas.

- The position of the words on the page surprised me. I thought the poem would be set out in stanzas, and I tried to make my version more regular.
- I thought that the original poem had movement in it that was like the movement in the print. My version didn't have that at all. The bit in the poem about the gown slipping over her shoulder really looked like the picture because of the shape of the lines.
- The line lengths made you pause and think about the way the words were connected. The poem was very reflective, and the lines made you respond to that.
- The ending of the original poem is ambiguous. Does she not open or is it the folded petals that she doesn't want to open?
- I like the way that 'She' and 'He' form lines of their own at the end of the poem. It made me think about the two people in the print, and what their positions and expressions might mean.
- I noticed patterns in the poem much more, like the colours that there are, and the repetition of her and his, and he and she. I noticed that because the poem started with 'They' and moved through 'he' and 'she' to 'One'. This made me think about how they were not really together.
- The poem seemed to me to be about power in the relationship, and the placing of the words made me wonder who really had the power here.
- I tried to make my version more ordered and regular, but that meant I lost the fluid shape of the original, and also its ambiguity.

In all the above comments the students were writing about form and structure. They wrote about the way the placing of words affects meaning and impact. They realised that what the poet works with is not just the words themselves, but also their **sounds**, their **patterns**, and their **positions**. Because they tried to impose a shape themselves, they became aware of how important it is to think about the ways the words look on the page.

Look at another poem now. This one is by Edward Thomas and was written during the First World War.

No one so Much as You

No one so much as you loves this my clay,
Or would lament as you its dying day.
You know me through and through though I have not told,
And though with what you know you are not bold.

None ever was so fair as I thought you:
Not a word can I bear spoken against you.
All that I ever did for you seemed coarse
Compared with what I hid nor put in force.

Scarce my eyes dare meet you lest they should prove
I but respond to you and do not love.
We look and understand, we cannot speak
Except in trifles and words the most weak.

I at most accept your love, regretting
That is all: I have kept a helpless fretting
That I could not return all that you gave
And could not ever burn with the love you have,

Till sometimes it did seem better it were
Never to see you more than linger here
With only gratitude instead of love –
A pine in solitude cradling a dove.

(Edward Thomas)

Commentary

Let's think about what the poet is saying here. He is writing about a one-sided relationship, and feels – what? Guilt? Sorrow? Resignation? Pity?

His language reflects his feelings, though the words chosen are simple, even spare (think about the effects of choice of language). One or two words stand out in this – like the final image, and perhaps the word 'burn' because they form a contrast to the simplicity and directness of the rest of the language.

What about the **form** and **structure** of the poem? Each stanza deals with an aspect of the relationship. The last two stanzas are linked together because they form one sentence; otherwise each stanza is self-contained. There are rhyming couplets which link lines, ideas and feelings together. This gives the feeling perhaps of containing the pain which the poet is writing about.

This is a brief discussion that attempts to link together the content of the poem with its form and structure. But the poem we have just examined briefly is not the poem that Thomas wrote. The words are the same, and in the same order, but he set them out differently. Look now at the real poem:

No one so Much as You

No one so much as you
Loves this my clay,
Or would lament as you
Its dying day.

You know me through and through
Though I have not told,
And though with what you know
You are not bold.

None ever was so fair
As I thought you:
Not a word can I bear
Spoken against you.

All that I ever did
For you seemed coarse
Compared with what I hid
Nor put in force –

Scarce my eyes dare meet you
Lest they should prove
I but respond to you
And do not love.

We look and understand
We cannot speak
Except in trifles and
Words the most weak.

I at the most accept
Your love, regretting
That is all: I have kept
A helpless fretting

That I could not return
All that you gave
And could not ever burn
With the love you have,

Till sometimes it did seem
Better it were
Never to see you more
Than linger here

With only gratitude
Instead of love –
A pine in solitude
Cradling a dove.

(Edward Thomas)

How is this different from the poem you looked at before? Think about the way it works when it is shaped like this.

This version seems emotionally less contained and controlled. The rhyming couplets have gone, and now every other line rhymes. This makes the poem more jagged, less unified. Because the word 'burn' is placed at the end of a line, we notice it more. (This shows the interlinking of word choice and form and structure.)

The splitting of the last line means that we see more of separation between the 'pine' and the 'dove'. The poem now seems more of a series of individual statements, as if the poet is working out his feelings, or is unwilling to admit them to himself. The pain of the poem is emphasised, rather than any resignation. In the third stanza, the separation of the first two lines stresses that he 'thought' she was fair: the short lines emphasise the fact that this was in the past, and is no longer true.

In the fifth stanza there is a gap between 'respond' and 'love' since they are on separate lines. This reinforces the gap between the feelings of the poet and the woman to whom he is addressing the poem.

This is not a comprehensive discussion, but it should point you in the direction of **analysing** and **evaluating** the effects of the form of this poem. You must avoid using words such as 'flowing' when you talk about form and structure. You have to be precise, and to **link** the lines, words, feelings and ideas.

Patterns and sounds

In order to consolidate what has been discussed about these techniques, let's examine another poem.

The Voice

Woman much missed, how you call to me, call to me,
Saying that now you are not as you were
When you had changed from the one who was all to me,
But as at first, when our day was fair.

Can it be you that I hear? Let me view you, then,
Standing as when I drew near to the town
Where you would wait for me: yes, as I knew you then,
Even to the original air-blue gown!

Or is it only the breeze, in its listlessness
Travelling across the wet mead to me here,
You being ever dissolved to wan wistlessness,
Heard no more again far or near?

Thus I; faltering forward,
Leaves around me falling,
Wind oozing thin through the thorn from norward,
And the woman calling.

Thomas Hardy (1840–1928)

Commentary

If we apply to this poem some of the techniques discussed above, we can analyse the effects of this poem. Remember we are trying to think about *how* the poet's choices shape meaning, not just what we think the meaning is.

If you look at the words on the page, you will see a distinct difference between the last stanza and the previous three. The **pattern** of **rhyme** stays the same, in that every other line rhymes, but the verse has shorter, more broken lines. This disjointed form reflects the state of mind the poet wishes to convey: the word 'faltering' could be applied to the form of the poem too. And the 'f' **sound** is repeated in the words 'forward' and 'falling', linking these words together and stressing the feeling of uncertainty and sorrow. The word 'forward' might suggest progress, but is undermined by being linked with 'faltering' and 'falling'.

The rhyme of the first three stanzas is unusual since three syllables are used for rhyme. The word 'wistlessness' is apparently an invention by Hardy, and its sounds link it with 'listlessness'. The total effect is of a line dying away, as the poet realises the voice he has heard is not really there, and a mood of desolation is evoked. The linking of 'wan' with wistlessness by the initial sound (known as alliteration) adds to the atmosphere. Here we see sound and meaning yoked together.

The word order is unusual. Look, for example, at the third and fourth lines in the third stanza. What effect does this have? Sometimes, students assume that the word order in poetry is bound to be different, but this is not so. Hardy gives the effect here of awkwardness, of hesitation, of working out his feelings as he goes along. This ties in with the unusual language, but although this is the effect it is not true that the poem is not crafted and **shaped** or structured deliberately.

Remember that in a poem there is always a tension between the sentence structure and the line endings, since it is natural to pause slightly at the end of a line while reading, even though the sense of the sentence might well go on. If a poem is end-stopped, that is each line is a self-contained statement, the effect is quite different.

Now consider this poem:

To My Dear and Loving Husband

If ever two were one, then surely we.
If ever man were loved by wife, then thee;
If ever wife was happy in a man,
Compare with me ye women if you can.
I prize thy love more than whole mines of gold.
Or all the riches that the East doth hold.
My love is such that rivers cannot quench,
Nor ought but love from thee give recompense.
Thy love is such I can no way repay,
The heavens reward thee manifold I pray.
Then while we live, in love let's so persever,
That when we live no more, we may live ever.

Anne Bradstreet (1612–72)

Commentary

In this poem we can see that each line makes a separate statement, though is not necessarily a whole sentence. If we link this with the **repetition** of 'if ever' at the beginning of the first three lines, what we see is a regularity, reinforced by the repetition of the sounds at the beginning of the last four lines. Even without analysing the meaning of the language, we can see the pattern here of regularity, calm, even serenity, which fits in with the account of the relationship in the poem. The fact that the poem is not broken up into separate stanzas also creates an effect of solidity and unity.

KEY CONCEPTS

analysis	evaluate	form
link	pattern	position
repetition rhyme	shape	sound

3.3 Poetry in context

AQA A	U3
AQA B	U2
EDEXCEL	U1
OCR	U2
WJEC	U3
NICCEA	U1

The poems of Philip Larkin (1922–1985) are set by WJEC, Edexcel and AQA A. AQA B requires students to be aware of the context of the poetry (AO5i). Larkin was a writer whose work has been increasingly criticised in the years since his death particularly in the light of the publication of his letters, which revealed him to be (in the view of many readers) racist and sexist, as well as disdainful of the working classes. It may not be possible to disregard these attitudes when you read his poetry, though you may feel that his views written in letters are not relevant to an assessment of his poetry. This is an area which it is not easy to form a final opinion on, but it is important to be aware of the different views held by critics, and the reasons for those views.

Here is an extract from one of Larkin's most famous poems, *Whitsun Weddings* first published in 1964.

Whitsun Weddings

At first, I didn't notice what a noise
The weddings made
Each station that we stopped at: sun destroys
The interest of what's happening in the shade,
And down the long cool platforms whoops and skirls
I took for porters larking with the mails
And went on reading. Once we started, though,
We passed them grinning and pomaded, girls
In parodies of fashion, heels and veils,
All posed irresolutely, watching us go,

As if out on the end of an event
Waving goodbye
To something that survived it. Struck, I leant
More promptly out next time, more curiously,
And saw it all again in different terms:
The fathers with broad belts under their suits
And seamy foreheads; mothers loud and fat;
An uncle shouting smut; and then the perms,
The nylon gloves and jewellery-substitutes,
The lemons, mauves, and olive-ochres that

Marked off the girls unreally from the rest.
Yes, from cafés
And banquet-halls up yards, and bunting-dressed
Coach-party annexes, the wedding-days
Were coming to an end. All down the line
Fresh couples climbed aboard; the rest stood round;
The last confetti and advice were thrown,
And, as we moved, each face seemed to define
Just what it saw departing: children frowned,
At something dull; fathers had never known

Success so huge and wholly farcical;
The women shared
The secret like a happy funeral;
While girls, gripping their handbags tighter, stared
At a religious wounding. Free at last,
And loaded with the sum of all they saw,
We hurried towards London, shuffling gouts of steam.
Now fields were building-plots and poplars cast
Long shadows over major roads, and for
Some fifty minutes, that in time would seem

Just long enough to settle hats and say
I nearly died
A dozen marriages got under way.

Philip Larkin

Commentary

It is possible to discuss this poem in terms of its language, form and structure only, but it is hard to avoid commenting on the **values** and **attitudes** which underpin it. We have to be aware, of course, that at the time that Larkin was writing the details he uses would have been more part of everyday life. He has been accused of being patronising.

What is your response to the description of the girls 'grinning and pomaded', the fathers with their 'seamy foreheads', mothers 'loud and fat' and uncles 'shouting smut'?

When Larkin gives the actual words used: 'I nearly died', what is his tone?

The whole situation is probably unknown to you. Newly married couples no longer go on honeymoon by train, being seen off by their families. Therefore you can see that

context is important, and that context affects how we make meaning out of what we read. You can see from the above extract that the speaker in the poem is an outsider, an observer, and not all of the details observed will be familiar to you. But as well as **analysing** the tone, the form and the ideas in the poem, you should not be afraid to **evaluate**, to set a text in its wider context, to explore the idea of **values** and **attitudes** in the text.

You may come to the conclusion that these can be considered acceptable in the period in which the text was produced, but you should not make the assumption that everyone of the period would have thought the same way. Would a working-class, as opposed to a middle-class, writer have observed in that way? Larkin proclaims his status as an unmarried and childless man in his poems. How might this affect his views? He was conservative in his politics, and Oxbridge educated. He was, of course, male. A critic has commented on the way Larkin saw the working classes as wearing 'cheap ugly clothes'. You can see something of that attitude in the lines above. Do you mind these comments in the poems?

KEY CONCEPTS

analyse	attitude	context
evaluate	value	

3.4 Context and attitudes

AQA A	U3
AQA B	U2
EDEXCEL	U1
OCR	U2
WJEC	U3
NICCEA	U1

In the following poem by Carol Ann Duffy (born 1955) the writer addresses some of the issues about how we define 'English Literature'. What kinds of attitudes do you think she is mocking?

Head of English

Today we have a poet in the class.
A real live poet with a published book.
Notice the inkstained fingers girls. Perhaps
we're going to witness verse hot from the press.
Who knows. Please show your appreciation
by clapping. Not too loud. Now

sit up straight and listen. Remember
the lesson on assonance, for not all poems,
sadly, rhyme these days. Still. Never mind.
Whispering's, as always, out of bounds –
but do feel free to raise some questions.
After all, we're paying forty pounds.

Those of you with English Second Language
see me after break. We're fortunate
to have this person in our midst.
Season of mists and so on and so forth.
I've written quite a bit of poetry myself,
am doing Kipling with the Lower Fourth.

Right. That's enough from me. On with the Muse.
Open a window at the back. We don't
want winds of change about the place.
Take notes, but don't write reams. Just an essay
on the poet's themes. Fine. Off we go.
Convince us that there's something we don't know.

Well. Really. Run along now girls. I'm sure
that gave an insight to an outside view.
Applause will do. Thank you
very much for coming here today. Lunch
in the hall? Do hang about. Unfortunately
I have to dash. Tracey will show you out.

Carol Ann Duffy

Commentary

Here are some suggestions about the attitudes Duffy is mocking:

- She satirises the attitudes of old-fashioned English teachers who dislike 'winds of change'.
- She allows the *Head of English* to reveal her own prejudices in her own voice.
- References to 'Kipling' and the 'Muse' show her ideas about poetry.
- She also says that 'sadly' 'not all poems rhyme these days'.
- 'Seasons of mist and so on and so forth' reveals another of her definitions of poetry – Keats.
- She wants value for money: after all, they are paying 'forty pounds'.
- She reduces poetry to 'an essay on the poet's themes'.
- She is evidently offended by what the 'real life poet' has said: 'Well. Really.'
- She discourages too much enjoyment and engagement: 'Applause will do.'

It is likely that without some kind of **context** for this we would be unable to pick up the targets of satire. If we know that Duffy herself has given poetry readings, we will read the tone differently. It will also change our response if we are familiar with contrasting definitions of English Literature, or have met teachers with similar ideas. We also need to be aware of the context of **genre**, not just of the poem itself, but also of the idea of allowing a poem to be told in a voice which is definitely not the poet's own.

Context of an earlier poem

Let's look now at a seventeenth-century poem written by John Donne (1572–1631).

Why does he address the poem to the sun? And why in these terms?

How does the argument change?

Look at the big claims Donne is making in this stanza

The Sun Rising

Busy old fool, unruly sun,
Why dost thou thus,
Through windows, and through curtains call on us?
Must to thy motions lovers' seasons run?
Saucy pedantic wretch, go chide
Late school-boys, and sour prentices,
Go tell court-huntsmen, that the King will ride,
Call country ants to harvest offices;
Love, all alike, no season knows, nor clime,
Nor hours, days, months, which are the rags of time.

Thy beams, so reverend, and strong
Why shouldst thou think?
I could eclipse and cloud them with a wink,
But that I would not lose her sight so long:
If her eyes have not blinded thine,
Look, and tomorrow late, tell me,
Whether both the Indias of spice and mine
Be where thou left'st them, or lie here with me.
Ask for those kings whom thou saw'st yesterday,
And thou shalt hear, All here in one bed lay.

She is all states, and all princes I,
Nothing else is.
Princes do but play us; compared to this,
All honour's mimic; all wealth alchemy.
Thou sun art half as happy as we,
In that the world's contracted thus;
Thine age asks ease, and since thy duties be
To warm the world, that's done in warming us.
Shine here to us, and thou art everywhere;
This bed thy centre is, these walls, thy sphere.

John Donne

Commentary

You might be asked questions on the following topics on this poem (Open Book exam paper):

- the presentation of thoughts and feelings
- the kind of love that is shown in the poem
- comparisons and contrasts with other poems by Donne.

In this case you can see that **context** has been interpreted as the poem in the context of other poems by the same writer. But in order to make a meaningful reading of the poem, you will have to be aware of the context of the ideas of the time, the poetic conventions of the time, and your own responses in a twenty-first-century context.

The ideas in this poem are complex and the verse **structure** reflects this. Each stanza develops a different argument. The first one tells the sun to go elsewhere, and not disturb lovers who are outside time's limitations. The second points out that the speaker could 'eclipse' the sun by winking, and that all the riches and royalty of the world are in that bed. The third stanza develops the idea by saying that nothing else really exists except the lovers who diminish everything else considered valuable to fraud and pretence ('play', mimic', 'alchemy'). And the sun need go no further than that bed which is the centre of the cosmos.

Donne is at home with these ideas, and we are not. We have to have them explained in order to make an informed reading of the poem. This explanation is providing us with a **context** for the feelings and ideas in the poem. It would be wrong to assume that no other writer of the time used these ideas, but we could certainly pick up on the way that Donne blends together science and emotions. Here is a good starting point for comparing the poem with others written by the same poet.

The kind of love shown in the poem depends on **context** also. It is useful to analyse the attitude shown towards the woman in the poem. Is it an attitude that you can recognise and understand? Is it possible to say that love remains the same no matter what the period or situation? There is a kind of pride or possessiveness in this poem that perhaps strikes you as boastful or exaggerated. It may not be possible to find a modern equivalent. It may not also be possible to react in the same way if you are female. There is perhaps an assumption that the intended reader of the poem is male, as is the writer. The issue of **gender** is important here, and this is also part of the **context** of the **reader**.

3.5 Voice

AQA A	U3
AQA B	U2
EDEXCEL	U1
OCR	U2
WJEC	U3
NICCEA	U1

Compare the Duffy poem we looked at earlier to one of U.A. Fanthorpe's (born 1929). Whose voice is she adopting?

The Sheepdog

After the very bright light,
And the talking bird,
And the singing,
And the sky filled up wi'wings,
And then the silence,

Our lads sez
We'd better go, then.
Stay, Shep. Good dog, stay.
So I stayed wi' t' sheep.

After they cum back,
It sounded grand, what they'd seen:
Camels, and kings, and such,
Wi'presents – human sort,
Not the kind you eat –
And a baby. Presents wes for him.
Our lads took him a lamb.

I had to stay behind wi' t' sheep.
Pity they didn't tek me along too.
I'm good wi' lambs,
And the baby might have liked a dog
After all that myrrh and such.

U.A. Fanthorpe

Commentary

What Fanthorpe does here is give the reader an unusual angle on a familiar story. The sheepdog belongs to the shepherds who went to see the baby Jesus. Fanthorpe gives the sheepdog dialect speech which sounds homely and northern. This fits in with the simple, even naïve, attitude shown by the sheepdog. The writer **foregrounds** the voice here by giving an animal human speech. She has chosen the humblest of creatures to express the wonder of the events. An angel is seen as 'the talking bird', and the lines 'It sounded grand, what they'd seen:/Camels, and kings, and such,' give dramatic but familiar events a new life. The same technique is applied to 'all that myrrh and such'.

Your response

How are you meant to feel? Surprised? Amused? Touched? Probably a mixture of all of these, along with other reactions depending on your own feelings about the original story. And the adopting of such an unusual voice is responsible for much of the response.

Both this poem and the Duffy poem were written in the twentieth century. Let's look at an extract from a nineteenth-century poem written by Tennyson (1809–1892).

Ulysses

It little profits that an idle king,
By this still hearth, among these barren crags,
Matched with an aged wife, I mete and dole
Unequal laws unto a savage race,
That hoard, and sleep and feed, and know not me.
I cannot rest from travel: I will drink
Life to the lees: all times I have enjoyed
Greatly, have suffered greatly, both with those
That loved me, and alone; on shore, and when
Thro' scudding drifts the rainy Hyades
Vext the dim sea. I am become a name;
For always roaming with a hungry heart
Much have I seen and known, cities of men
And manners, climates, councils, governments,
Myself not least, but honoured of them, all;
And drunk delight of battle with my peers,
Far on the ringing plains of windy Troy.
I am a part of all that I have met;
Yet all experience is an arch wherethro'
Gleams that untravelled world, whose margin fades
For ever and for ever when I move.
How dull it is to pause, to make an end,
To rust unburnished, not to shine in use!
As tho' to breathe were life. Life plied on life
Were all too little, and of one to me
Little remains, but every hour is saved
From that eternal silence something more,
A bringer of new things; and vile it were
For some three suns to store and hoard myself,
And this grey spirit yearning in desire
To follow knowledge, like a sinking star
Beyond the utmost bound of human thought.

Alfred, Lord Tennyson

What is his attitude?

What does he want?

Questions

- What kind of voice is created here?
- What use is made of the classical background?
- What attitude does the speaker adopt?
- What comments can you make on the language and images?

Commentary

Ulysses (Greek name Odysseus) was absent from his home Ithaca for twenty years, at Troy, and then journeyed home (his 'Odyssey'). He longed to return home to his wife and son, but Tennyson presents us with a Ulysses who feels unfulfilled, and yearns for further adventure. He thought he would be content when he returned home but finds himself dissatisfied, and still yearning for further adventure:

> I will drink
> Life to the lees:

He longs to be useful still:

> To rust unburnished, not to shine in use!

Both these images present the reader with a picture of desire to live, and live with some purpose. He wants to drink his wine right to the dregs, to experience everything, to leave nothing. And he fears the consequences of a dull life, which leads to 'rust', as when a tool or a weapon is not used but merely abandoned.

Although he is old, he still wants more:

> And this grey spirit yearning in desire
> To follow knowledge, like a sinking star
> Beyond the utmost bound of human thought.

He sees no need to settle for the life he is now living: adventure and experience are still within his spirit.

Tennyson is making use of a story, assumed to be familiar to his readers, to comment on old age, perhaps in a more universal way. We can link this poem to the situation of anyone used to an active and fulfilled life who does not want to settle for less. The **rhythm** of the poem, with its **iambic pentameter**, lends weight to the feelings and thoughts in it. The lines consist of five sets of two syllables, with the second one stressed. A **trochaic metre** (stressed, unstressed) would sound much less serious:

> Hubble, bubble, toil and trouble
> Fire burn and cauldron bubble

as the witches say in *Macbeth*; sounds like a spell. And think back to the Hardy poem with its three syllable rhymes. This rhythm is **dactylic** – stressed followed by two unstressed syllables – and gives much more sense of a falling or dying away, which is in keeping with Hardy's mood and subject matter. While it is not essential that you know this terminology, you should be able to analyse the reasons for the patterns of sound effects, their link with the subject matter and their impact.

KEY CONCEPTS

dactylic	foregrounding	iambic pentameter
rhythm	trochaic metre	

3.6 Form as genre

AQA A	U3
AQA B	U2
EDEXCEL	U1
OCR	U2
WJEC	U3
NICCEA	U1

Another way of defining the form of a poem is to define which poetic **genre** it belongs to. We have already looked at **dramatic monologues**, where the poet uses a voice decidedly not their own. The object of adopting another voice might be to satirise the speaker, or to allow them to reveal their own nature for us to criticise, as in the Duffy poem. Or it might be to allow us to think about a situation in another way, as Fanthorpe does with the sheepdog voice. We are given an unusual angle on a story we are familiar with. The poet thus **defamiliarises** the story. It is important to recognise, however, the fact that all poems are written in a voice that we cannot with certainty say is the writer's own. The poet adopts a **persona**, or mask to write behind, although sometimes it is much more overt and direct than others. So don't assume that all poetry is straight-from-the-heart feelings. Be aware that the process of **shaping** necessarily puts a distance between the writer and the poem.

There are poetic forms that are long-established, with their own rules and conventions. Sonnets are one example. We'll now look at two sonnets, the first by Shakespeare, and the second by William Wordsworth.

Sonnet 130

My mistress' eyes are nothing like the sun;
Coral is far more red than her lips' red;
If snow be white, why then her breasts are dun;
If hair be wires, black wires grow on her head.
I have seen roses damasked, red and white,
But no such roses see I in her cheeks,
And in some perfumes is there more delight
Than in the breath that from my mistress reeks.
I love to hear her speak, yet well I know
That music hath a far more pleasing sound.
I grant I never saw a goddess go;
My mistress when she walks treads on the ground.
And yet, by heaven, I think my love as rare
As any she belied with false compare.

Shakespeare (1564–1616)

Shakespeare is not simply working within the conventions of a sonnet, (in this case the form of what is now known as a Shakespearean sonnet), but also responding to previous examples of sonnets. **Intertextuality** is an important concept here. Texts do not and cannot stand alone. They refer back to other texts, deliberately or not, and in turn influence later ones. In this case Shakespeare is reacting to conventional portraits of women in poems of his time which elevated the woman to a position of goddess.

The structure of the poem is important. The sonnet is in three groups of four lines with a concluding final couplet, which sums up and rounds off the ideas in it. Although the rhyming words are different in each group of four lines, the **pattern** is the same. And, of course, the last two lines rhyme, which both separates them from the rest of the poem and links them together. Each group of four lines deals with a separate aspect of the woman's appearance, and develops the argument further.

Now compare the Shakespeare sonnet with this poem by Wordsworth:

It is a beauteous Evening

It is a beauteous Evening, calm and free;
The holy time is quiet as a Nun
Breathless with adoration; the broad sun
Is sinking down in its tranquillity;
The gentleness of heaven is on the Sea:
Listen! the mighty Being is awake,
And doth with his eternal motion make
A sound like thunder – everlastingly.
Dear Child! dear Girl! that walkest with me here,
If thou appear'st untouched by solemn thought

> Thy nature is not therefore less divine:
> Thou liest in Abraham's bosom all the year;
> And worship'st at the Temple's inner shrine,
> God being with thee when we know it not.
>
> William Wordsworth (1802)

The structure of this sonnet is different. It makes more sense to see it as two groups of eight lines, followed by six, and the **rhyme scheme** is what signals this to us. The two four line sets rhyme a-b-b-a, and the six line a-b-c-a-b-c. Therefore, there is much less sense of the developing argument ready to be concluded by a two line overview. Instead, the writer moves from the scene he is describing to the woman he is walking with, linking the two with his sense of God being within here, even unawares. There is a feeling of the presence of God in the 'beauteous evening' and this is shown in the choice of words such as 'nun', 'holy' and 'heaven'. You can see that the form, structure and choice of language all work together.

KEY CONCEPTS

defamiliarise	dramatic monologue	genre
intertextuality	persona	rhyme scheme

3.7 Choice of language

AQA A	U3
AQA B	U2
EDEXCEL	U1
OCR	U2
WJEC	U3
NICCEA	U1

Although we have looked at the effects of choice of language in every section of this chapter, here is a task designed to draw your attention very specifically and directly to the effects of choice of words and phrases. The poem was written by Robert Frost (1874–1963):

> Snow falling and night fading fast, oh, [ ]
> In a field I looked into going past,
> And the ground almost covered [ ] in snow
> But a few weeds and stubble showing [ ].
>
> The woods around it have it – it is [ ].
> All animals are smothered in their [ ]
> I am too [ ] to count;
> The loneliness includes me [ ].
>
> And lonely as it is that [ ]
> Will be more [ ] ere it will be less –
> A blanker whiteness of [ ] snow
> With no expression, nothing to [ ].
>
> They cannot [ ] me with their empty spaces
> Between stars – on stars where no [ ] is.
> I have it in me so much nearer [ ]
> To scare myself with my own [ ] places.
>
> Robert Frost

A very good way of understanding the effects of the choice of language is to fill these gaps. Your version will be very different, and you will be more aware of the **connotations** of particular words. That is, all the associations they carry with them. You will also focus on the sounds of words, and the patterns that they make.

Have a go at filling in the gaps now.

Here is a version of the first stanza made by a student who tried this task.

> Snow falling and night fading fast, oh, [*heavenly*]
> In a field I looked into going past,

And the ground almost covered [*thickly*] in snow
But a few weeds and stubble showing [*below*].

And here is the first stanza of the original poem.

Snow falling and night fading fast, oh, fast
In a field I looked into going past,
And the ground almost covered smooth in snow,
But a few weeds and stubble showing last.

The student's comments follow.

I did have a rhyme in my version, but I made the last two lines rhyme. Frost has three lines rhyming, then the one that doesn't fit in with the rest which makes the poem more eerie and mysterious. I lost the repetition of 'fast' in the first line which meant I also lost the repeated 'f' sound in the first two lines. And an 's' sound went too because I chose 'thickly' instead of 'smooth'. But 'fast' being repeated gives a sense of speed and movement which my version didn't have. His version sounds sadder than mine because of these sounds, and this fits in with the last verse which is all about sadness and fear and desolation within yourself.

You can see in the student's comment an awareness that sounds, patterns and meanings all fit together in shaping effects and responses. This is an important feature to be aware of, and will help all the time in informing your comments about form, structure and language.

Here is the rest of the poem:

The woods around it have it – it is theirs.
All animals are smothered in their lairs.
I am too absent-spirited to count;
The loneliness includes me unawares.

And lonely as it is that loneliness
Will be more lonely ere it will be less –
A blanker whiteness of benighted snow
With no expression, nothing to express.

They cannot scare me with their empty spaces
Between stars – on stars where no human race is.
I have it in me so much nearer home
To scare myself with my own desert places.

Robert Frost

Sample question and model answer

Practice and consolidation

See if you can apply all that you have learned to an evaluation of student responses to the following question on a poem.

Read the following poem then answer all the questions.

From *Sonnets from the Portuguese:*

How do I love thee? Let me count the ways.
I love thee to the depth and breadth and height
My soul can reach, when feeling out of sight
For the ends of Being and ideal Grace.
I love thee to the level of everyday's
Most quiet need, by sun and candle-light.
I love thee freely, as men strive for Right;
I love thee purely, as they turn from Praise.
I love thee with the passion put to use
In my old griefs, and with my childhood's faith.
I love thee with a love I seemed to lose
With my lost saints, – I love thee with the breath,
Smiles, tears of all my life! – and, if God choose,
I shall but love thee better after death.

Elizabeth Barrett Browning

(i) How does the writer seek to impress her lover with the power of her love?
(ii) Write about the effectiveness of the repetition of 'I love thee' in this poem.
(iii) Selecting at least two more poems from this collection, explore the different methods Elizabeth Barrett Browning uses to express her feelings.

Look at these two answers to (ii). Which is better and why?

Answer A

Each time the poet says 'I love thee', she develops the 'ways' in which she loves such as 'freely', 'purely' and 'with...passion'. She starts the poem with the phrase as a question, and concludes it by extending her love to after death, so there is a sense that this love is eternal, and links back to her early life too: because the passion was 'put to use/In my old griefs, and with my childhood's faith'. She connects this love with God as well as morally good actions, such as when she refers to men who 'strive for right'. She uses words such as 'soul' and 'saints' which show how this love is religious in its nature. The phrase 'I love thee' forms an essential part of the structure of the poem; it provides the framework for a kind of list of the ways she loves, which she is counting, and its repetition has the effect of adding seriousness, weight and conviction each time it is repeated.

Answer B

The repetition of 'I love thee' is important because it helps the reader to understand that she loves this man a lot. The more times she says it, the more it seems truthful. It also helps the poem to flow. She starts off by saying she loves him, and goes on to say the different ways in which she does. There are religious words in the poem which suggest that she feels their love is holy, and she does talk about life after death. The more often she says she loves him, the more we believe her.

Sample question and model answer (continued)

Now look at the mark scheme for this question as a whole. Where would you put each answer, and why? We will focus on AO3: **show detailed understanding of the ways in which writers' choices of form, structure and language shape meanings.**

Band 1 0–5 marks:

few (if any) formal structural language features identified
very limited (if any) discussion of how language shapes meaning.

Band 2 6–10 marks:

some awareness of how form/structure/language shape meaning
some awareness of implicit meanings and attitudes.

Band 3 11–15 marks:

awareness of writer's technique and its influence on meaning
comment on some features of form, structure, language.

Band 4 16–20 marks:

recognition of authorial means in form, structure and language
evidence of how language choices shape meanings.

Band 5 21–25 marks:

detailed comments on how form, structure, language shape meanings
comments on the effectiveness of language choices.

Band 6 26–30 marks:

recognition of technique and features of form, structure, language
commentary on how form, structure, language shape meanings.

Commentary

Answer A

The comments are detailed, with some recognition of techniques. The answer is supported by reference to the text. Form, structure and language are interlinked, and there is considerable awareness of the ways in which meaning is shaped. Although this is only part of a whole answer, we would certainly, according to these criteria, be looking at the top band.

Answer B

The candidate here is reluctant to engage with the text. He doesn't quote, although there are references to the language. There is some awareness of attitudes, although the comments are not developed and supported. There are comments on language, but the candidate seems unwilling or unable to discuss form and structure. On this evidence, we would probably be looking at band 1, though there might be possibilities with this candidate to reach band 2.

In this chapter, we have focused on the importance of assessment objectives, and the key idea of how form, structure and language shape meaning. We have looked at responses of different readers, showing how you can use them to shape and inform your own responses. We have examined poetry of various kinds and periods, showing how you can apply techniques of analysis to many different poems of different types and periods.

We have discussed poetry set by all of the exam boards.

LEARNING SUMMARY

Exam practice and analysis

[Open Book]

Question

The Canterbury Tales: *The General Prologue* (Chaucer)

Refer to the portrait of the Pardoner in the *General Prologue* (lines 669–714) and comment on how it illustrates Chaucer's approach in introducing us to the character.

In your answer you should refer to the following aspects:

- physical and moral impression given of the character
- ways in which Chaucer shapes the reader's response
- use of historical and religious background.

[based on OCR]

AOs targeted: AO1, AO2i, AO3, AO4, AO5i

Notes

All the AOs are targeted here, with a particular emphasis on context,

AO1: depends on ability to construct a clear and sustained argument with textual reference

AO2i: need to show understanding of generic features, and how Chaucer conveys values and attitudes. Focus on 'moral' via 'physical' important here

AO3: need to explore Chaucer's presentation, the ways he introduces the information about the Pardoner:

- appearance
- voice
- job
- morality
- what he carries

there should be a focus on 'shape' here, and on irony in tone.

AO4: judgement and interpretation needed here.

AO5i: specifically addressed in bullet point 3 in question, with particular need to be aware of place of Church and religion of the time.

Chapter 4

Pre-twentieth-century prose

After studying this chapter you should know about:

- *place of assessment*
- *different kinds of questions*
- *narrative techniques, dialogue, description*
- *structure*
- *context*
- *right and wrong way to answer a question*

LEARNING OBJECTIVES

4.1 Assessment

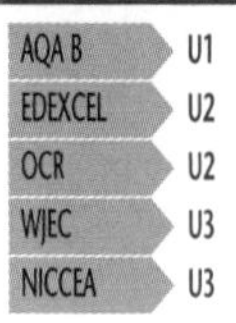

These are the texts set by the different boards, and the assessment objectives targeted:

AQA A

No pre-twentieth-century prose on AS syllabus

AQA B

AOs 1: 10%; 2i: 5%; 3: 5%; 4: 5%; 5i: 5%
Open Book

Thomas Hardy: *Tess of the D'Urbervilles*
Charles Dickens: *Great Expectations*
Jane Austen: *Pride and Prejudice*

EDEXCEL

AOs 1: 5%; 2i: 5%; 3: 5%, 4: 5%; 5i: 10%
Closed Book

Jane Austen: *Emma*
Charles Dickens: *Hard Times*
Thomas Hardy: *Return of the Native*
Mary Shelley: *Frankenstein*
Henry James: *Washington Square*

OCR

AOs 1: 10%; 2i: 10%; 3: 10%; 4: 5%; 5i: 5%
Open Book

Bram Stoker: *Dracula*
Jane Austen: *Persuasion*
Elizabeth Gaskell: *Mary Barton*
Charlotte Brontë: *Jane Eyre*

In addition, OCR offers a free choice of text in the coursework.

WJEC

AOs 1: 10%; 2i: 20%; 3: 10% Open Book

Jane Austen: *Emma*
Oscar Wilde: *The Picture of Dorian Gray*
Thomas Hardy: *The Mayor of Casterbridge*
Kate Chopin: *The Awakening and Selected Stories*
George Eliot: *The Mill on the Floss*

NICCEA

AOs 1: 10%; 4: 10%; 5i: 10%

Some are recommended texts but others can be chosen.

The Gothic novel
The rise of the novel
The Victorian novel
The Irish 'Big House' novel
19th-century American fiction

You will remember the importance of the assessment objectives in the study of AS and A Level English Literature. They determine the kinds of questions asked and the way that the answers are assessed.

If we take a text that occurs in more than one syllabus, we can look at the different kinds of questions that might be asked about it, and see how best to tackle them.

Let's start with Emily Brontë's *Wuthering Heights*. The emphasis on AOS will determine the style of the question and the way that your answer is marked.

You must also remember that the questions will be different depending on whether the exam is Open Book or not. The tasks will be different in their scope and approach if you have access to your text in the exam. In this case, both boards have set Open Text exams for pre-twentieth-century prose, but it is possible to use this to demonstrate different styles of questioning.

Let's take an example. Here is the opening of Emily Brontë's *Wuthering Heights*:

Chapter 1

1801

I have just returned from a visit to my landlord – the solitary neighbour that I shall be troubled with. This is certainly a beautiful country! In all England, I do not believe that I could have fixed on a situation so completely removed from the stir of society. A perfect misanthropist's heaven: and Mr. Heathcliff and I are such a suitable pair to divide the desolation between us.

A capital fellow! He little imagined how my heart warmed towards him when I beheld his black eyes withdraw so suspiciously under their brows, as I rode up, and when his fingers sheltered themselves, with a jealous resolution, still further in his waistcoat, as I announced my name.

'Mr. Heathcliff!' I said.

A nod was the answer.

'Mr. Lockwood, your new tenant, sir. I do myself the honour of calling as soon as possible after my arrival, to express the hope that I have not inconvenienced you by my perseverance in soliciting the occupation of Thrushcross Grange: I heard yesterday you had had some thoughts – '

'Thrushcross Grange is my own, sir,' he interrupted, wincing. 'I should not allow any one to inconvenience me, if I could hinder it – walk in!'

The 'walk in' was uttered with closed teeth, and expressed the sentiment, 'Go to the deuce': even the gate over which he leant manifested no sympathising movement to the words; and I think that circumstance determined me to accept the invitation: I felt interested in a man who seemed more exaggeratedly reserved than myself.

When he saw my horse's breast fairly pushing the barrier, he did put out his hand to unchain it, and then sullenly preceded me up the causeway, calling, as we entered the court – 'Joseph, take Mr. Lockwood's horse; and bring up some wine.'

'Here we have the whole establishment of domestics, I suppose,' was the reflection suggested by this compound order. 'No wonder the grass grows up between the flags, and cattle are the only hedge-cutters.'

Joseph was an elderly, nay, an old man: very old perhaps, though hale and sinewy. 'The lord help us!' he soliloquised in an undertone of peevish displeasure, while relieving me of my horse: looking meantime, in my face so sourly that charitably conjectured he must have need of divine aid to digest his dinner, and his pious ejaculation had no reference to my unexpected advent.

Wuthering Heights is the name of Mr. Heathcliff's dwelling. 'Wuthering' being a significant provincial adjective, descriptive of the atmospheric tumult to which its station is exposed in stormy weather. Pure bracing ventilation they must have up there at all times, indeed; one may guess the power of the north wind blowing over the edge, by the excessive slant of a few stunted firs at the end of the house; and by a range of giant thorns all stretching their limbs one way, as if craving the alms of the sun. Happily, the architect had foresight to build it strong: the narrow windows are deeply set in the wall, and the corners defended with large jutting stones.

Before passing the threshold, I paused to admire a quantity of grotesque carving lavished over the front, and especially about the principal door; above which, among a wilderness of crumbling griffins and shameless little boys, I detected the date '1500',

> and the name 'Hareton Earnshaw'. I would have made a few comments, and requested the history of the place from the surly owner; but his attitude at the door appeared to demand my speedy entrance, or complete departure, and I had no desire to aggravate his impatience previous to inspecting the penetralium.

A question which is based on the assumption that candidates have their text with them in the exam is likely to ask candidates to refer to a particular part of the text, and to re-read it before answering. A Closed Book exam is more likely to ask general questions, based on an overview of the text.

Possible question format

Here are examples of the two styles:

Question A

Re-read the opening pages of the first chapter of *Wuthering Heights*, up to 'the penetralium'. Then answer all parts of the question:

(i) What do we learn of Mr Lockwood in this extract?
(ii) Examine the ways in which Emily Brontë introduces us to Heathcliff here.
(iii) How does Brontë make use of the appearance of buildings here and in the rest of the novel?

Question B

What use does Emily Brontë make of different narrative techniques in the novel?

You can see that the first question requires a close reading of part of the novel. It is likely that in the real exam paper the questions would be based on a longer sequence from the novel. But this shows you something of the kinds of questions you will be asked. You will see links in question A with the style of questioning you might well be familiar with from your GCSE exams.

You should bear in mind that all modules will test AO1: knowledge, understanding and insight; appropriate terminology and accurate and coherent written expression.

Let's think about the points that could be made about Lockwood, the narrator of this part of the novel, and the way that Heathcliff is introduced.

- Lockwood's **language** seems inflated and pompous: his sentence structure is convoluted, and his vocabulary over-ornate. The word 'penetralium' seems absurdly inappropriate. A word such as 'provincial' suggests the differences he feels between himself and the people of this district.
- He imagines himself as solitary and withdrawn, though later in the novel this is proved to be certainly not true.
- He obviously sees himself as artistic and cultured, noticing details of the architecture as he enters the house.
- He is judgemental and critical, and seems to feel he is not treated properly by Heathcliff or Joseph.

- He comments on the lack of servants in the household, again suggesting that the standards here are lower than he is used to.
- He sees parallels between himself and Heathcliff, though it is clear to the reader almost immediately that they are not alike, and this is made more and more obvious as the novel progresses.
- He talks too much, in comparison to Heathcliff who is much more abrupt.

These are just some of the points which might be made about the **presentation** of Lockwood at the beginning of the novel.

What about Heathcliff?

- Lockwood describes his 'black eyes' which 'withdraw so suspiciously under their brows'. He is already seen in association with the word 'black', a description developed later in the novel.
- He is seen in **contrast** to the much more talkative and pompous Lockwood.
- Lockwood describes him as 'surly', and we can see he is unwelcoming and ungracious.
- He is evidently sensitive about his ownership of Thrushcross Grange. Thus, right at the beginning of the novel, ownership of property is **foregrounded**.
- Lockwood comments that the surroundings make this place a 'misanthropist's heaven'. And this suggests that we can draw the conclusion that Heathcliff has withdrawn deliberately from society.
- The differences between Heathcliff and Lockwood ironically are emphasised by the fact that Lockwood sees them as similar. This is very probably not the reader's perception of the two men.
- There is already an air of mystery about Heathcliff, as the reader's curiosity is aroused.

You can see from the comments above that another possible question would have been about the ways in which the reader's first view of Heathcliff is shaped and developed in the novel.

Even with such a limited extract from a long novel, it is possible to examine the language and come to conclusions about the way that the novel is being shaped. Questions often ask you to move from the particular to the general, and to broaden your answer to include further episodes from the text.

Selection is the key to this. You must not waste your time describing or narrating events from the novel, since this will not give you a pass grade. You need to refer to specific incidents to support your views.

KEY CONCEPTS

contrast	foregrounding	form
language	presentation	structure

4.2 Techniques

AQA B	U1
EDEXCEL	U2
OCR	U2
WJEC	U3
NICCEA	U3

One feature that arises in the above passage from *Wuthering Heights,* and question B, is that of **narrative techniques**. This is an important technique which needs careful thought and exploration. Sometimes students think that it is enough to say that **first person narrative** gives us an insight into a character's thoughts and feelings, and so makes us more sympathetic towards them, whereas with **third person narrative** we feel more distanced. However, this is much too much of a generalisation, and in this and the following chapter on prose we will be looking at this in greater detail.

We can see, for example, in the extract from *Wuthering Heights* that, although it is written in the first person, we are not invited to be particularly sympathetic towards Lockwood. In fact, Brontë goes on to use other first person narrators, setting one against the other, and giving us different views of the leading characters. She makes the reader feel insecure in their judgement perhaps, because it is hard to feel that we can rely on any single narrator. It is wrong to assume that we always feel we can identify with the narrator: often we can feel more sympathy and identification with a leading character when a novel is written in the third person, particularly if events are seen through their eyes. The question of **narrative point of view** is crucial in shaping our response to a text, and is something we shall keep returning to in these chapters.

ASSESSMENT OBJECTIVES

You will remember that AO4 requires you to articulate your own **independent judgements** informed by **other readers' views**. You always need to be aware that there are many different ways of reading a text. It is not possible to agree with all of them. 'Informed' is crucial here. You must not simply read a critic, and pass off their views as your own. That is why it is essential to listen to and read differing critical views, and then decide what you yourself think. You need to learn to develop confidence in your own judgement, and then your reader will find your point of view more convincing.

Critics' views

Here, for example, are some critics' views on *Wuthering Heights*. The novel has been seen:

- in terms of its patterns of imagery
- in terms of its narrative strategies
- as a moral fable
- as morally ambiguous
- as a tragic romance
- as a Gothic novel
- as a novel preoccupied with boundaries and divisions
- as written by Branwell Brontë, since a woman such as Emily could never have written it
- as a feminist critique of *Paradise Lost*
- in comparison to other novels written at the same time
- as a unique and timeless creation
- as a novel about class divisions
- as an analysis of the effects of property
- as an allegory of Irish history
- as a critique of British imperialism
- as an analysis of sexual roles
- as an argument for the desirability of death
- as a revelation of Victorian domestic violence
- as an exploration of women's powerlessness
- as subversive
- as not subversive
- as demonstrating the female desire for an impossible object
- as tracing the emergence of the modern family.

Heathcliff has been seen at different times by different critics:

- as an evil genius
- as an elemental figure
- as secondary in interest to Catherine
- as a representation of repressed desires

- as the embodiment of sexual energy
- as representing mythical man
- as a rebel against the values of civilisation
- as rootless, and with no place in society
- as an example of alienation
- as a representative of dispossessed Irish people
- as a savage outsider.

Each reading has to **foreground** some aspects of the novel, and to let other parts fade into the background. In many ways, the worst mistake a student can make in preparing for an A Level exam in English Literature, is to read one critical book, and assume that it contains the 'right' answer about a text. There is no such answer, and you should be prepared to present different views about texts. Critics have different agendas, and much recent criticism is related to the **context** of the work.

The same text can be interpreted in different ways, as you can see, but this does not mean that only one interpretation is correct, but that there are many ways of reading a text. What you should be is confident in your views, and **informed**.

KEY CONCEPTS

context	first person narrative	foreground
narrative point of view	narrative techniques	third person narrative

4.3 Dialogue

AQA B	U1
EDEXCEL	U2
OCR	U2
WJEC	U3
NICCEA	U3

Writers reveal to us characters and relationships through their use of dialogue. Let's look now at extracts from two Jane Austen novels.

In the first extract from *Pride and Prejudice*, Elizabeth Bennet is visiting the home of Mr Charles Bingley. His sisters, Miss Bingley and Mrs Hurst, and Mrs Hurst's husband, Mr Hurst, are present, as is Bingley's friend, Mr Darcy. Elizabeth is visiting because her sister Jane who is staying with the Bingleys, is ill.

> Elizabeth was so much caught by what passed, as to leave her very little attention for her book; and, soon laying it wholly aside, she drew near the card-table, and stationed herself between Mr. Bingley and his eldest sister, to observe the game.
>
> 'Is Miss Darcy much grown since the spring – ?' said Miss Bingley: 'will she be as tall as I am?'
>
> 'I think she will. She is now about Miss Elizabeth Bennet's height, or rather taller.'
>
> 'How I long to see her again! I never met with anybody who delighted me so much. Such a countenance, such manners, and so extremely accomplished for her age! Her performance on the pianoforte is exquisite.'
>
> 'It is amazing to me,' said Bingley, 'how young ladies can have patience to be so very accomplished as they all are.'
>
> 'All young ladies accomplished! My dear Charles, what do you mean?'
>
> 'Yes, all of them, I think. They all paint tables, cover screens, and net purses. I scarcely know any one who cannot do all this; and I am sure I never heard a young lady spoken of for the first time, without being informed that she was very accomplished.'
>
> 'Your list of the common extent of accomplishments,' said Darcy, 'has too much truth. The word is applied to many a woman who deserves it no otherwise than by netting a purse or covering a screen; but I am very far from agreeing with you in your estimation of ladies in general. I cannot boast of knowing more than half-a-dozen in the whole range of my acquaintance that are really accomplished.'
>
> 'Nor I, I am sure,' said Miss Bingley.
>
> 'Then,' observed Elizabeth, 'you must comprehend a great deal in your idea of an accomplished woman.'
>
> 'Yes; I do comprehend a great deal in it.'

'Oh, certainly,' cried his faithful assistant, 'no one can be really esteemed accomplished who does not greatly surpass what is usually met with. A woman must have a thorough knowledge of music, singing, drawing, dancing, and the modern languages, to deserve the word; and, besides all this, she must possess a certain something in her air and manner of walking, the tone of her voice, her address and expressions, or the word will be but half deserved.'

'All this she must possess,' added Darcy; 'and to all she must yet add something more substantial in the improvement of her mind by extensive reading.'

'I am no longer surprised at your knowing only six accomplished women. I rather wonder now at your knowing any.'

'Are you so severe upon your own sex as to doubt the possibility of all this?'

'I never saw such a woman. I never saw such capacity, and taste, and application, and elegance, as you describe, united.'

Mrs. Hurst and Miss Birgley both cried out against the injustice of her implied doubt, and were both protesting that they knew many women who answered this description, when Mr. Hurst called them to order, with bitter complaints of their inattention to what was going forward. As all conversation was thereby at an end, Elizabeth soon afterwards left the room.

'Eliza Bennet,' said Miss Bingley, when the door was closed on her, 'is one of those young ladies who seek to recommend themselves to the other sex by undervaluing their own; and with many men, I daresay, it succeeds; but, in my opinion, it is a paltry device, a very mean art.'

'Undoubtedly,' replied Darcy, to whom this remark was chiefly addressed, 'there is meanness in all the arts which ladies sometimes condescend to employ for captivation. Whatever bears affinity to cunning is despicable.'

Miss Bingley was not so entirely satisfied with this reply as to continue the subject.

Commentary

For most of this novel, we see events through Elizabeth's eyes. Here, though, Austen gives the reader a chance to see what happens when Elizabeth is not present. The fact that Miss Bingley speaks about Elizabeth 'when the door was closed on her' suggests that she immediately and eagerly seizes the opportunity to criticise her.

In the dialogue which precedes this, we can see that we are being presented with a kind of competition between the two women for Darcy's approval. Or at least that is how Miss Bingley perceives it. Notice how Miss Bingley echoes Darcy's remarks in her desire to win his attention and approbation. Austen calls her 'his faithful assistant'. In contrast, Elizabeth does not mind disagreeing with Mr Darcy: her attitude is much less reverential. She takes him less seriously, and the reader is aware that this is exactly the attitude which will appeal more to Darcy.

We can see even in a brief extract that Miss Bingley is not going to succeed. Darcy's remarks to her are an indirect insult, and the narrator's comment that Miss Bingley 'was not so entirely satisfied with this reply as to continue the subject' shows us that Miss Bingley is nothing like as quick-witted as Elizabeth. Her desperation to win Darcy's favours, we sense, is always going to be counterproductive. But her desire to diminish Elizabeth in his eyes by deliberately misinterpreting Elizabeth's remarks is unlikely to gain the reader's sympathy, and it is quite clear that Austen is herself not presenting Miss Bingley to us in order to gain that sympathy. There is some quite complex interaction here, given with a few clues from the narrator. In particular she uses the **contrast** between Miss Bingley and Elizabeth, and the moment when Elizabeth leaves the room confirms the reader's views about the two women, as it is intended to. Elizabeth refuses to conform to Darcy's stereotype of an 'accomplished woman', and her cool remarks make Miss Bingley's comments sound silly and exaggerated.

The **irony** of the narrator's last comment about Miss Bingley leaves us in no doubt that intelligence is a significant **value** here.

In the second extract, from Austen's *Emma*, Emma Woodhouse and several others are on an outing to a local beauty spot. Frank is a friend of Emma's, and Miss Bates is a local, unmarried and relatively poor woman. Mr Knightley is an old friend of the Woodhouse family. Frank and Emma have been flirting.

> 'It will not do,' whispered Frank to Emma, 'they are most of them affronted. I will attack them with more address. Ladies and gentlemen, I am ordered by Miss Woodhouse to say, that she waives her right of knowing exactly what you may all be thinking of, and only requires something very entertaining from each of you, in a general way. Here are seven of you, besides myself (who, she is pleased to say, am very entertaining already), and she only demands from each of you, either one thing very clever, be it prose or verse, original or repeated; or two things moderately clever; or three things very dull indeed; and she engages to laugh heartily at them all.'
>
> 'Oh! very well,' exclaimed Miss Bates; 'then I need not be uneasy. "Three things very dull indeed." That will just do for me, you know. I shall be sure to say three dull things as soon as ever I open my mouth, shan't I?' (looking round with the most good-humoured dependence on everyone's assent).
>
> 'Do you not all think I shall?'
>
> Emma could not resist.
>
> 'Ah! ma'am, but there may be a difficulty. Pardon me, but you will be limited as to number – only three at once.'
>
> Miss Bates, deceived by the mock ceremony of her manner did not immediately catch her meaning; but when it burst on her, it could not anger, though a slight blush showed that it could pain her.
>
> 'Ah! Well – to be sure. Yes I see what she means,' (turning to Mr Knightley) 'and I will try to hold my tongue. I must make myself very disagreeable, or she would not have said such a thing to an old friend.'

Commentary

In both these extracts the writer is revealing to us through dialogue the interactions of the society she is describing. And in both, we know how to make judgements of the characters because of the techniques of the writer, even though no judgement is given directly to us.

In the extract from *Emma*, for example, we can see that Miss Bates is in a sense at the mercy of the two younger people. They conspire together to make her feel excluded: Frank 'whispered' to Emma. They are entertaining themselves at the expense of someone more vulnerable than themselves. Frank instigates, but Emma rises to the bait readily. If we contrast the ways in which Emma and Miss Bates speak, we can see that we are likely to judge Emma for her cruel mockery. This is set out in the following table:

Emma	*Miss Bates*
Only requires something very entertaining from each of you	though a slight blush showed that it could pain her
Could not resist	deceived
ma'am	I must make myself very disagreeable
Pardon me, but you will be limited as to number – only three at once	the most good-humoured dependence on everyone's assent
the mock ceremony of her manner	I will try to hold my tongue to an old friend

You can see from this table that when you set the words and actions and motives of one character against the other, Austen has stressed the good nature of Miss Bates, hurt and not altogether comprehending, against the sharper, but in this case malicious Emma. And we know more about Emma than we do about Miss Bates. Emma 'could not resist': we understand something of her motives. But we are looking at Miss Bates from the outside: 'a slight blush showed that it could pain her'. This **narrative point of view** positions the reader and enables them to form opinions about the characters.

Even from such a brief extract we can see the significance of this incident, and this arises from the way Austen **presents** it to us. In this case, although Emma has the intelligence, the **value** implied by the presentation of the scene is that it must be tempered by kindness, and in particular kindness for the more vulnerable members of this society. That is, a society within limits, since Miss Bates by the standards of the time in England was undoubtedly well off. But in this society she survives only by the help of others – material and social.

The **mood** of both pieces is different. The **ironic narrative voice** of the first extract is not present in the second.

KEY CONCEPTS

contrast	ironic narrative voice	irony
mood	narrative point of view	presentation
value		

Possible question format

A sample Open Book question on *Emma*, set by OCR, asks the candidate to discuss Jane Austen's 'presentation and development of relationships' in the chapter as a whole. Then relate this to Austen's narrative methods in the novel as a whole.

The idea of moving from a part to a whole is typical of an Open Book question. One thing you have to keep in focus here is the necessity to divide your time effectively, so that you don't spend too much of your time on the extract. In this case, the topic is a very broad one, so the answer will depend on **focus** and **selection of textual detail** in support of the argument.

4.4 Description

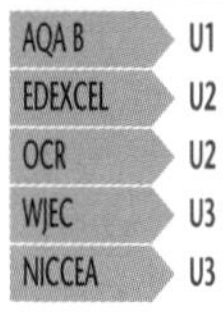

Here is the opening of *Hard Times* by Charles Dickens (1854).

Chapter 1

The One Thing Needful

'Now, what I want is, Facts. Teach these boys and girls nothing but Facts. Facts alone are wanted in life. Plant nothing else, and root out everything else. You can only form the minds of reasoning animals upon Facts: nothing else will ever be of any service to them. This is the principle on which I bring up my own children, and this is the principle on which I bring up these children. Stick to Facts, Sir!'

The scene was a plain, bare, monotonous vault of a schoolroom, and the speaker's square forefinger emphasized his observations by underscoring every sentence with a line on the schoolmaster's sleeve. The emphasis was helped by the speaker's square wall of a forehead, which had his eyebrows for a base, while his eyes found commodious cellarage in two dark caves, overshadowed by the wall. The emphasis was helped by the speaker's mouth, which was wide, thin and hard set. The emphasis was helped by the speaker's voice which was inflexible, dry, and dictatorial. The emphasis was helped by the speaker's hair, which bristled on the skirts of his bald head, a plantation of firs to keep the wind from its shining surface, all covered with knobs, like the crust of a plum pie, as if the head had scarcely warehouse-room for the hard facts stored inside. The speaker's obstinate carriage, square coat, square legs, square shoulders – nay, his very neckcloth, trained to take him by the throat with an unaccommodating grasp, like a stubborn fact, as it was – all helped the emphasis.

'In this life, we want nothing but Facts, sir; nothing but Facts!'

Look at Dickens's narrative methods here. What opinion do you think he wants you to have of the speaker, and what makes you think this?

Commentary

It is unlikely that you thought that you were meant to like or approve of the speaker, but how does Dickens make you respond in this way? Here are some suggestions about the ways in which Dickens uses **description** to influence the reader's opinions:

- No name is given to 'the speaker' (who is thus depersonalised)
- Repetition of phrases such as 'the emphasis was helped by', and 'the speaker' (gives us the effect of a list, and also perhaps suggests the speaker's own pompous and repetitive way of speaking).
- Repetition of words such as 'square' (fits in with the stress on 'facts').
- Sustained images: the speaker's forehead is a 'square wall' and his eyes are set in 'two dark caves overshadowed by the wall' (the effect is of lack of light, of darkness of feature and thought). The speaker's hair 'bristled' on his bald head, and the image is sustained as it is compared to a 'plantation of firs' put there to shelter the 'shining surface' of the bald head. Then the head is compared to 'the crust of a plum pie'; then to a warehouse of facts (the images are funny, strange and all unpleasant).
- Choice of adjectives, such as 'obstinate', 'unaccommodating' and 'stubborn'; and 'wide, thin and hard set' and 'inflexible, dry and dictatorial' (notice that these last are given to us in sets of three, a typical persuasive device).
- The setting: a 'plain, bare, monotonous vault of a schoolroom' (sounds designed to cram in facts and to stifle creativity, and also uses a set of three).
- The structure of the opening as we move from the speech, to the setting to the speaker's appearance (we can connect all these parts together, so that the writer creates a total picture of a particular attitude towards education, which by association becomes unattractive and even laughable).

If you can examine a passage in this way, you are applying **analytical** methods: that is, you are not just giving an account of the content, but you are exploring the writer's **techniques** and **effects**.

Contrast this extract with another one taken from *Great Expectations* by Charles Dickens (1861):

> My sister, Mrs Joe, with black hair and eyes, had such a prevailing redness of skin, that I sometimes used to wonder whether it was possible she washed herself with a nutmeg grater instead of soap. She was tall and bony, and almost always wore a coarse apron, fastened over her figure behind with two loops, and having a square impregnable bib in front, that was stuck full of pins and needles. She made it a powerful merit in herself, and a strong reproach against Joe that she wore this apron so much. Though I really see no reason why she should have worn it at all; or why, if she did wear it at all, that she should not have taken it off every day of her life.

Commentary

You can see differences between this description and the previous Dickens extract. For one thing, the narrative voice here is that of a boy, not a third-person narrator. Except it is the grown-up narrator (Pip) looking back at the child's views, but inevitably filtered by an adult's perspective. The vocabulary is an adult's, and of course, you have to be aware that 'Pip' – child or adult – is in any case a **construct** and not a real person. The **values** here need sorting out. At some points in the novel it is the voice of the adult narrator reflecting on the feelings and actions of his younger self; sometimes it is the child's values we are meant to accept.

In this case, the adult and child seem to be agreed in their judgement of Pip's sister, Mrs Joe.

Look at these words and phrases:

- black hair and eyes

- a prevailing redness of skin
- tall and bony
- a coarse apron
- a square impregnable bib
- stuck full of pins and needles.

What is the impression that these add up to?

It seems to me that we have a picture of aggression, of what is intended to be an unfeminine woman. The child Pip wonders why she will not remove her apron, and we are bound to take his view on this. The picture is of an unattractive, bossy, martyred woman who resents her life. The association of the 'nutmeg grater' and the 'pins and needles' suggests sharpness and possible violence, even though they are ordinary household objects. The reader's responses are **shaped** by the writer, and the reader may well be manipulated into sharing the writer's **values**. Our sympathies are likely to be with Pip, since he is remembering his childhood, when his situation is one of relative weakness and vulnerability.

Let's examine another extract from a set text, this time from *Jane Eyre*, by Charlotte Brontë (1847). This extract comes from the first chapter of the novel. Jane is an orphan in the household, and John Reed is the spoiled son of the widowed Mrs Reed. Her late husband undertook to take care of the orphaned Jane.

In this extract we also have the child's eye view, filtered through an adult's perception. How are we meant to perceive John Reed?

What is the effect of these underlined words and phrases?

> John Reed was a schoolboy of fourteen years old; four years older than I, for I was but ten; large and stout for his age, with a dingy and unwholesome skin; thick lineaments in a spacious visage, heavy limbs and large extremities. He gorged himself habitually at table, which made him bilious, and gave him a dim and bleared eye with flabby cheeks. He ought to have been at school; but his mamma had taken him home for a month or two, 'on account of his delicate health'. Mr Miles, the master, affirmed that he would do very well, if he had fewer cakes and sweetmeats sent him from home; but the mother's heart turned from an opinion so harsh and inclined rather to the rather more refined idea that John's sallowness was owing to over-application, and, perhaps, to pining after home.

Commentary

The **presentation** of the character of John is bound to influence our opinion here. Here are some words and phrases I have selected:

- large and stout
- thick lineaments
- heavy limbs
- gorged himself
- dim and bleared eye
- sallowness
- dingy and unwholesome skin
- spacious visage
- large extremities
- bilious
- flabby cheeks

Brontë's choice of language gives the reader a picture of a large and unhealthy boy, unhealthy because of his greed. Notice how his size is emphasised. Why do you think it might be?

Since their relative ages are stressed, we can see that he is in a position of **power** over Jane. The differences between ten and fourteen are considerable. Brontë wishes us to feel pity and empathy for the child Jane, who is being confronted, and in this section of the novel, bullied by an older, bigger and more powerful boy. Placing the comment about the age difference before the description of John is an essential part of the **structure** of this piece of writing. And Brontë follows up the description by references to John's mother's false idea of her son, and her over-indulgence of him. Introducing a brief piece of direct speech, evidently from his 'mamma', reinforces our impressions of a spoiled bully.

> What I have tried to show you here is how to **analyse** a passage, not just to explain it, or to describe it. You need always to bear in mind AO3: **show detailed understanding of the ways in which the writer's choices of form, structure and language shape meanings.** It is not enough either to give a 'character study' of the type you may have been used to at GCSE. It is essential that you examine how the writer achieves her effects – the **presentation**.
>
> ASSESSMENT OBJECTIVES

Now look at another extract from *Jane Eyre*. This time the narrator is the adult Jane, who is seeing for the first time the mad wife of her employer, Mr Rochester, the man she was meant to be marrying.

> He lifted the hangings from the wall, uncovering the second door, this, too, he opened. In a room without a window, there burnt a fire guarded by a high and strong fender, and a lamp suspended from the ceiling by a chain. Grace Poole bent over the fire, apparently cooking something in a saucepan. In the deep shade, at the farther end of the room, a figure ran backwards and forwards. What it was, whether beast or human being, one could not, at first sight tell: it grovelled, seemingly on all fours; it snatched and growled like some strange wild animal: but it was covered with clothing, and a quantity of dark, grizzled hair, wild as a mane, hid its head and face.
>
> ...
>
> The lunatic sprang and grappled his throat viciously, and laid her teeth to his cheek: they struggled. She was a big woman, in stature almost equalling her husband, and corpulent besides: she showed virile force in the contest – more than once she almost throttled him, athletic as he was. He could have settled her with a well-planted blow, but he would not strike: he would only wrestle.

Commentary

Although there is little direct comment from Jane, the narrator, the whole situation, along with the writer's choice of language makes the reader horrified by what Jane now sees. The secrecy of what we are told about is important: the second door is 'uncovered' so that the reader realises that some dreadful secret is to be revealed. At first what is revealed seems relatively harmless, then follows the description of the 'figure', referred to as 'it' rather than she at first. The aimless movement of the figure is unpleasant. The verbs 'grovelled', 'snatched' and 'growled' all serve to dehumanise the woman.

Notice that Brontë makes Jane not know whether it is a 'beast or human being', but places 'beast' first, so that influences our reactions, since we are seeing events through Jane's eyes. The likeness of a woman to an animal is stressed and developed. And when she is allowed her humanity, what is then emphasised is her size and masculinity. She is 'a big woman', almost as big as her husband. She is 'corpulent'. Compare this to the description of John Reed earlier in the novel. Brontë uses relative sizes as part of her narrative techniques. She shows 'virile force' in the struggle with her husband. He, however, in **contrast** to her wild behaviour, displays restraint and a kind of 'gentlemanliness' in his refusal to 'strike' and settle her.

Although Mrs Rochester (who is not named) has physical power, she has no power to fight the situation. Contrast this with the situation of the young Jane, who was relatively weak and powerless against the older more privileged John. Yet we are not being encouraged to sympathise with the 'mad' woman in any way here. Our sympathies are with the silent observer, Jane. Mrs Rochester is distanced from us, and there is no possible way that we could identify with her or even recognise her humanity, because of the way she is **presented**.

At the end of this chapter are two responses to a question on *Jane Eyre*. In the responses to these answers, the points about analysis of presentation will be further developed.

analysis	construct	contrast
description	effect	presentation
shape	structure	technique
values		

KEY CONCEPTS

4.5 Structure

AQA B	U1
EDEXCEL	U2
OCR	U2
WJEC	U3
NICCEA	U3

We have examined the structure of individual extracts, but it is also necessary to look at the structure of whole texts. *Jane Eyre*, for example, is structured round the early life of Jane. *Great Expectations* tells the story of Pip, from childhood to adulthood. However, the structure is more complex than this might suggest. Think about the following questions.

Progress check

Refer to the text you are studying and answer these questions.

- How much time does the novel cover?
- What does it leave out?
- What periods are particularly focused on?
- At what point does it begin?
- At what point does it end?
- What age does the narrator seem to be at the time of the telling?
- Is there a significant turning point in the text?
- What use is made of different settings?
- What important stages does the leading character go through?
- What changes and developments does he/she undergo?
- What patterns and parallels can you find in different sections of the text?
- What time difference is there between the events and the telling?

These are all suggestions which will help you to decide on the structure of the novel. Which of these suggested questions are relevant to a novel told in the first person?

Commentary

The key questions are the sixth (What age does...) and the last (What time difference...). And these are connected to the **narrative point of view**. We have already looked at the adult/child split in the narrative voice of *Jane Eyre* and *Great Expectations*. Since many first-person novels concern themselves with the growth and changes of the narrator, this double perspective is crucial.

But narrative structure can be seen in many ways. Let's take *Jane Eyre* as an example. This should show you how you can think about some of the points above when you are commenting on the effects of structure.

Gateshead

In the novel *Jane Eyre*, the leading character, Jane, is first introduced to the reader at the age of ten. The events within the novel focus on a relatively small number of sequences in her life. The first section of the novel is set in Gateshead, the home of the Reeds. We see what happens to Jane when she defies John Reed and his mother. So the events cover only a few days.

Lowood

Then Jane is sent to school at Lowood. There is intense focus on the first weeks at Lowood, and the events and relationships that influence Jane. Chapter 9 in the novel deals swiftly with the passing of time – from January to June. After the death of a friend, however, clearly a key incident in Jane's life, the narrator announces: 'I now pass a space of eight years almost in silence'.

Thornfield

At eighteen, Jane takes a post as governess at Thornfield, home of Mr Rochester. A chapter is given to Jane's decision to find a job, and the ways in which she sets about it. A further chapter tells us about the transition from Lowood to Thornfield. But the months from October, when Jane arrives, to January, when Rochester arrives home, occupy only one further chapter, signalling the importance of this event.

The following six months which Jane spends at Thornfield, take a further 17 chapters, out of the novel's total of 38. This is obviously crucial in Jane's life as it concerns her growing love for Rochester, culminating in his proposal of marriage, and the dramatic revelation of his mad wife, locked in the attic. During these months, some time is spent describing Jane's return to Gateshead to see the death of Mrs Reed, and for her to discover what happened to the Reed children. Their lives form a kind of **parallel** to hers, and take up just over one chapter.

Moor House

After the discovery of Mrs Rochester, Jane flees Thornfield and finds refuge at Moor House with the Rivers family – two sisters and a brother. There is a transition chapter as Jane wanders starving before they take her in. The Rivers family forms a contrasting **parallel** to the Reeds, also two sisters and a brother. Six chapters of the novel are devoted to the time with the Rivers family, which takes a year of Jane's life. However, most time is spent on Jane's arrival at the house, and then on her resistance to St John Rivers' proposal of marriage. The discovery that they are her cousins, and that she has inherited money is important, but not as important as the interaction with St John.

Ferndean

There is another transition chapter as Jane returns to Thornfield in search of Mr Rochester, then redirects her search to another house, Ferndean. One chapter deals with Jane's reunion with Rochester, and the final chapter covers ten years of Jane's married life, explaining briefly what has happened to the Rivers family.

This brief outline should show you that the **structure** of a novel is very deliberately shaped to focus the reader on the key events, feelings and ideas of the leading character's life. You could pick up ideas such as the significance of place names, which in this case seem to represent stages in Jane's life. But it is essential that you don't assume that equal attention is paid to all parts of the life created for us.

Progress check

You can summarise the key movements and events of the novel you are studying in the way I have done here. This will enable you to understand the process of **selection** and **presentation** in the structure, and its effects on the reader.

Comparison with Frankenstein

Here is a short extract from Mary Shelley's novel *Frankenstein* (1818). It comes from the first part of the novel. It is part of a letter written by Robert Walton, who is on an ice-bound ship near Archangel in Russia, to his sister, Margaret Saville, in England. The novel begins with three of these letters, all quite short. This account then follows.

What effect do you think this narrative technique has?

> He then told me he would commence his narrative the next day when I should be at leisure. This promise drew from me the warmest thanks. I have resolved every night, when I am not imperatively occupied by my duties, to record, as nearly as possible in his own words, what he has related during the day. If I should be engaged, I will at least make notes. This manuscript will doubtless afford you the greatest pleasure, but to me, who know him, and who hear it from his own lips, with what interest and sympathy shall I read it in some future day!
>
> Even now as I commence my task, his full-toned voice swells in my ears; his lustrous eyes dwell on me with all their melancholy sweetness; I see his thin hand raised in animation, while the linearments of his face are irradiated by the soul within. Strange and harrowing must be his story; frightful the storm which embraced the gallant vessel on its course, and wrecked it – thus!

Commentary

Here is where you can see the way that the **structure** of the novel and the **narrative point of view** work together. The reader's curiosity is aroused by the description of the man who seems to combine suffering and charisma. We want to know the events that have caused this. But at the same time, Shelley effectively **distances** us from the events. The narrative is not at first hand, nor even second hand. It is a transcription of a spoken account, sent as part of a letter. And although we might find the events of the plot improbable, Shelley has given them a kind of **context**, since they are being sent to a woman in London, so we are both drawn in, and held at a distance.

It is always important to analyse the effects of such narrative choices.

Endings

You have looked at the beginning of novels, so let's look at the effects of an ending. This is the ending of *Tess of the D'Urbervilles* by Thomas Hardy (1891).

> 'Justice' was done, and the President of the Immortals, in Aeschylean phrase, had ended his sport with Tess. And the d'Urberville knights and dames slept on in their tombs, unknowing. The two speechless gazers bent themselves down to the earth, as if in prayer, and remained thus a long time, absolutely motionless: the flag continued to wave silently. As soon as they had strength they arose, joined hands again, and went on.

This is a commentary on tragic events in the novel. You can see by the classical **allusions** that Hardy wishes to emphasise the parallel with Greek tragedy, with his references to the 'President of the Immortals' and 'Aeschylean phrase'. The idea of the gods having 'sport' with human beings is a common one in literature. The **mood** is quiet and calm. There is almost a sense of reverence as the 'silent gazers' bend 'as if in prayer'. The scene is very still. It follows a death, an execution, though this is not described directly to us.

Hardy both distances us by his comments on the events of the novel, and involves us, by the profound sense of sorrow and inevitable injustice. His references to Greek tragedy reminds us that the Greeks saw humanity as at the mercy of the gods, and Hardy in a way universalises Tess' experiences, although the novel has been the story of one woman's life.

allusion	context	distance
mood	narrative point of view	parallel
presentation	selection	structure

4.6 Context

AQA B	U1
EDEXCEL	U2
OCR	U2
WJEC	U3
NICCEA	U3

The Awakening by Kate Chopin was published in 1899. Look at this extract from it.

Look at the effect of the underlined phases.

> She let herself in at the gate, but instead of entering she sat upon the step of the porch. The night was quiet and soothing. All the tearing emotions of the last few hours seemed to fall away from her like a sombre, uncomfortable garment, which she had but to loosen to be rid of. She went back to that hour before Adele had sent for her; and her senses kindled afresh in thinking of Robert's words, the pressure of his arms, and the feeling of his lips on her own. She could picture at that moment no greater bliss on earth than possession of the beloved one. His expression of love had already given him to her in part. When she thought that he was there at hand, waiting for her, she grew numb with the intoxication of expectancy. It was so late; he should be asleep perhaps. She would awaken him with a kiss. She hoped he would be asleep that she might arouse him with her caresses.
>
> Still, she remembered Adele's voice whispering, 'Think of the children, think of them.' She meant to think of them, that determination had driven into her soul like a death wound – but not to-night. To-morrow would be time to think of everything.
>
> Robert was not waiting for her in the little parlour. He was nowhere at hand. The house was empty. But he had scrawled on a piece of paper that lay in the lamplight:
>
> 'I love you. Good-bye-because I love you.'
>
> Edna grew faint when she read the words. She went and sat on the sofa. Then she stretched herself out there, never uttering a sound. She did not sleep. She did not go to bed. The lamp sputtered and went out. She was still awake in the morning, when Celestine unlocked the kitchen door and came in to light the fire.

Why is context important here?

Commentary

The writer is showing us very explicitly the passionate feelings of a married woman with her lover. There is a stress on the physical, and we know that she has left her children to be with him. Her desolation at the end of this extract is understated. It is what is left unsaid that has the effect on the reader, as much as what is said.

The change in Edna's emotions is conveyed by the lack of description of her feelings at the end of the extract. Instead, a series of short sentences describe her actions.

The writer's choice of language earlier shows the intensity of her love for Robert. The previous emotion was like 'a sombre uncomfortable garment' that she has got rid of. Her senses 'kindled' as she remembers his caresses. The **connotations** of 'kindled' are of fire and burning, all traditional images used to describe love. Her state is compared to 'intoxication' and the exaggeration of 'no greater bliss on earth' shows the extent and nature of her love.

We can analyse and evaluate this passage, but what we can also do is to set it in its context – published just over a hundred years ago.

One of the questions set by an exam board (Edexcel) on this text picks up on this point:

Possible question format

Either: **(a)** When it was first published in 1899, *The Awakening* was attacked for being 'sordid and immoral'. Is this how it seems to you as a modern reader?

Or: **(b)** What qualities and features seem to you typical of the writer of this collection?

The second question (b) is not focused on this assessment objective (AO5i), but the first one (a) depends on a consideration of **context**.

You will need to think about the impact of the language and subject matter on readers of the time. It is likely that the way the text was received then was very different from what it would be now. Such frankness in describing a married woman's love for another man would cause no shocks now, but when this text appeared, it was attacked by critics. The **gender** of the writer is another factor. Because it was written by a woman, and many of the critics were male, we can see that issues about stereotypes of appropriate behaviour are very much dependent on the context of the time.

Thomas Hardy also faced criticism for the frank discussion of sexual matters in his novels, but the age both he and Chopin lived in (though Chopin is American and Hardy English) judged women more harshly. In fact, Chopin was a critical failure, selling very few books, and having subsequent works rejected by publishers.

It was not until the 1960s that Chopin's work was rescued from oblivion, showing us that critical judgements can vary a great deal from age to age. The **reception** of literature is an area of some academic study in recent years, and it is true that the reaction to writing can vary according to the period, and the gender, race or class of writer, amongst other factors. Edna's desire for freedom may have different resonances for different readers.

KEY CONCEPTS

connotation context focus
gender reception

ASSESSMENT OBJECTIVES

All this is relevant to AO5i: (the context of writer **and** reader), but also to AO4 (where you need to think about other reader's interpretations).

Sample question and model answer

Practice and consolidation

Here is a question on Charlotte Brontë's *Jane Eyre*, with extracts from two responses to it.

Remind yourself of Chapter 1, from "Boh! Madam Mope!" cried the voice of John Reed' (about three pages in) to the end of this chapter.

Use this extract as a starting-point to discuss Brontë's presentation of Jane's suffering here and at one other point in the novel.

The extract named includes the first section from the novel discussed earlier. Here are the two responses.

Answer A

John Reed is not a pleasant character. He bullies Jane, and takes advantage of her position in the household. He is described in terms which stress his greed and ill health. Brontë refers to his 'flabby cheeks' and 'unwholesome skin'. We feel sorry for Jane because of John's behaviour. John's mother obviously spoils him, and he is allowed to do whatever he wants. He is large and heavy, and used to getting his own way.

Commentary

Although there are several relevant comments here, with textual support, can you see the real problem with this response?

What Candidate A has done is to focus almost exclusively on the character of John. He has supported these comments which move beyond character study, into some aspects of presentation. However, there is no real **focus** in this answer on what the question demands, which is 'Jane's suffering'. By the end of this extract we are into a 'character study'. It would have been more helpful to put the words 'large' and 'heavy' in inverted commas, since they are quotations from the text, and this would signal to the examiner that the text was being used effectively and confidently.

Answer B

Charlotte Brontë emphasises Jane's powerlessness in this part of the novel. She is at John's mercy, and we realise it takes a great deal of courage to stand up to him. We know that John's mother always over-indulges him, through the very unattractive picture that Brontë gives us. He is described in terms which stress his greed and ill health. Brontë refers to his 'flabby cheeks' and 'unwholesome skin'. The focus here is on their relative positions. Jane cannot retaliate and receive justice. Brontë first says that John is four years older than Jane, who is 'but ten'. The fact that this occurs before the description of the bullying increases the impression of Jane as alone and a victim of John. Later in the novel Jane suffers at the hands of St John Rivers, who, although a religious man and unlike John in many ways, still uses his superior power to try to make her do what he wants. The description of St John stresses his whiteness and coldness, contrasting to the description of the large, heavy John, with his 'dim and bleared eye'.

Commentary

Why is this response better? Here, the candidate has addressed the question much more securely. She moves from this extract to another quite skillfully, rather than

Sample question and model answer *(continued)*

simply discussing this extract, then moving on to another. Whilst the latter is acceptable as an approach, the one in B seems more confident, and evaluative. She links together parts of the text, pointing out patterns and contrasts. Her analysis is more assured and focused. Quotations are integrated clearly and helpfully.

You can see that even analysis is not adequate if that analysis is not specifically directed to the task.

LEARNING SUMMARY

In this chapter, we have looked at pre-twentieth-century prose. Mostly you will be assessed on this by exam, though it is also possible to write on this in coursework. All of the skills covered here are applicable to both exam and coursework.

The importance of the assessment objectives has been stressed, with discussion of how these might be applied to the texts. All the texts discussed have been taken from the AS Level specifications of the various exam boards.

There has been a focus on different narrative techniques, with practical examples for consideration. Students' work has been discussed and evaluated.

We have looked at a number of exam questions, and suggested responses, bearing in mind different styles of question depending on the various assessment objectives targeted, and whether the exam is Open or Closed Book.

Exam practice and analysis

[Open Book]

Question

Jane Eyre (Charlotte Brontë)

Remind yourself of the section of Chapter 10 which begins 'I went to my window, opened it and looked out' to 'I got up and took a turn in the room, undrew the curtains, noted a star or two, shivered with cold, and again crept to bed.'

Using this as a starting point, discuss Brontë's presentation of the idea of freedom and independence in the novel.

AOs targeted: AO1, AO2i, AO3

Notes

This is an Open Book exam, so there must be close reference to the chosen passage. The key is moving from the passage to the novel as a whole, and making links between the two.

AO1: argument, reference to narrative techniques

AO2i: showing understanding of pre-twentieth-century prose

AO3: focus on 'freedom and independence' and on 'presentation'. Detailed references to different sections of the novel, not just narrative:

- financial freedom
- confinement
- work
- spiritual freedom
- freedom to love
- contrast to Bertha
- contrast to the Reeds
- strong language of the passage – e.g. 'servitude'
- structure, different stages of the novel
- ending and Jane's free choice.

Chapter 5

Twentieth-century prose

After studying this chapter you should know about:

LEARNING OBJECTIVES

- *the place of assessment*
- *narrative techniques*
- *narrative voices*
- *significance of context*
- *right and wrong way to answer a question*

5.1 Assessment

AQA A U1
AQA B U1
OCR U2
WJEC U2

These are the texts set by the different boards, and the assessment objectives targeted:

AQA A

AOs 1: 7%; 2i: 10%; 3: 8%; 4: 5% Closed Book

Charles Frazier: *Cold Mountain*
Michael Frayn: *Spies*
William Golding: *The Spire*
A.S. Byatt: *Possession*
Angela Carter: *Wise Children*

AQA B

AOs 1: 15%; 2i: 5%; 3: 8%; 4: 5% Open Book

F. Scott Fitzgerald: *The Great Gatsby*
Arundhati Roy: *The God of Small Things*
Alice Walker: *The Color Purple*
Graham Swift: *Waterland*

NICCEA

No twentieth-century prose set

EDEXCEL

No twentieth-century prose set

OCR

AOs: 1: 10%; 2i: 10%; 3: 10%; 4: 5%; 5i: 5% Open Book

Joseph Conrad: *Heart of Darkness*
E.M. Forster: *A Passage to India*
Raymond Carver: *Short Cuts*
Julian Barnes: *A History of the World in 10½ Chapters*

WJEC

AOs: 1: 5%; 3: 5%; 4: 20% Open Book

Emyr Humphries: *A Toy Epic*
Pat Barker: *Regeneration*

ASSESSMENT OBJECTIVES

We will be using several of the above texts in order to explore the techniques needed to achieve the assessment objectives. You should bear in mind, though, that even if the texts discussed are not ones you are actually studying, the comments made are intended to apply to all the twentieth-century prose texts you are studying, for coursework as well as exam.

5.2 The short story

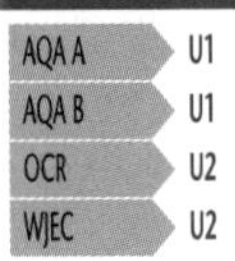

As a starting point in this chapter, we are going to consolidate the ideas and techniques of the previous chapter by using a short story to exemplify some of the techniques and effects you will need to be familiar with.

Look at this short story by Jane Gardam, taken from *The Pangs of Love* (1983).

An Unknown Child

The bandaged della Robbia babies stretched their arms in blessing towards the piazza. Across the piazza the Englishwoman sat on a high window seat of the pensione and looked at them in the autumn evening light.

Her husband said, 'Come for dinner.'

'It's a wonderful evening. Look at the della Robbia babies. It's a pity about the traffic in between.'

'They'll want us to be in time for dinner. It's a pensione.'

'I'm glad the della Robbias are still there. They were there when I was twenty.'

'They were there when your grandmother was twenty. And her grandmother. And hers. We ought to go in for dinner.'

'Yes. Wait. I'm glad they haven't hacked them off the walls yet. They took the frescoes off the walls you know. Some sort of blotting paper. We'll see the marks where they used to be tomorrow. When I was here you could actually touch the frescoes. With your hands. Just going down the street. Like in the Renaissance. They survived the war but not the tourists. I'm glad they haven't hacked off the babies.'

Every bit of the journey there had been babies. From London to Calais, Calais to Milan, Milan to Florence. A baby had watched them from the next quartet of seats on the Inter-city. Babies had screamed and chatted and roistered and roared, been carried and rocked and coaxed and shouted at on the boat. Larger, older ones had rushed about the deck, pushed their heads over the side between the spume and the sea-gulls, all the way to France. Two Swiss six-year-old babies with the heads of financiers had been absorbed in pocket calculators across the carriage from them all the way to the frontier. The night, from Switzerland to Chiasso, had been made sleepless by the wailing of an Umbrian infant with the toothache. From Milan, the corridor had been solid with nursing mothers.

He had said, 'Evelyn, why the hell are we not travelling first class?'

'I didn't last time.'

'My heaven – nearly twenty years ago. And you were fit then. You could have just about walked to Italy then.'

'I'm fit now,' she said. 'A miscarriage isn't an illness. It's usual. A blessing. We know it.'

He was a doctor. That her miscarriage of a child was a blessing was a fact that he had levelly insisted upon since it happened, two weeks ago. The child, he had told her, had certainly been wrong. For the rest of their lives they would have been saddled with –

She had lain on the bed and said nothing. They had been married twelve years. For fifteen she had been doing medical research, as busy as he in the same teaching hospital. On her marriage she had made it clear that she had no intention of wasting herself – her youth, her training – in childbearing. Her brain was at its best. Children could come later. Good heavens, you could have a child at forty now. There was that top Civil Servant woman who had had a child – perfectly healthy child – at fifty. It had always been so – able women often produced children late. Mrs Browning – (For Evelyn was properly educated: literary as well as medical.)

And she looked so young for her age. It had become a joke at parties, how young Evelyn stayed. 'I'm Mrs Dorian Grey,' she said, though few of Mick's colleagues knew what she meant. Mick had loved her first (it sounded crude) because of her health – her health, energy and bright eyes, and shiny seaside hair and out-spoken Yorkshire good sense. In a rare moment of imagination – it had made up her mind to him – he had called her 'The Scarborough Girl'. It had been her lovely, apparently indestructable youth and health and sense that had given him the courage to tell her at once after the miscarriage – directly after his consultation with her gynaecologist – that, at her age, there must be no more. To conceive a child again must be out of the question.

'Why?'

He told her. She listened thoughtfully, with a careful, consulting-room expression, not looking at him but at the waving top of the silver birch outside their bedroom window, for the miscarriage had taken place at home as they had so dashingly planned that the birth should do. The foetus had been between four and five months old. It had lain with her for an hour in the bed. It had had small limp arms. There was no telephone by the bed and she had waited an hour for him to get back from the hospital. The only sound in the empty house had been the whimpering and scratching of the dog at the bedroom door and her terrified, thumping heart fearing that it might get in. She had bled a good deal and had watched the birch tree turn its topmost leaves first one way and then the other in the evening light, had fainted as Mick arrived. As she fainted she had his eyes in a band of brightness, separate from seemed to see his face and filled with raw dismay. Afterwards – he had been so steady – she thought that this must have been a dream.

'I'm sorry,' he said now, 'I didn't know this place was opposite the Innocenti baby place. You should have let me book a good hotel. Just because you were here before – it's no good trying to live things over again.'

'I don't try. It's lovely here. I knew it would still be lovely, even with all the traffic now. When I was here before, the piazza used to be almost empty. In the early morning there'd be just one donkey and cart going across, and someone spreading out a flower stall round the feet of the statue. Now this huge great car park. But the light's the same. And the buildings – the columns of the orphanage.' 'Come and have dinner.'

'And along here,' she said, walking ahead of him down the narrow corridor with the old slit windows, 'the floor used to crackle with the heat as if the boards were on fire. 'And you could see mountainous great cedars – look. See them. Look. And just the top of the dome where the Michelangelo David is. Look how solid the trees are.'

'Oh - and the dining room's exactly the same. Exactly. Look. Pure E.M. Forster. There's even the same long table down the middle.'

They were shown, however, past the long table to one of the empty side tables. The long table, though fully laid, stayed empty.

'I was here twenty years ago,' she said to the waitress who exclaimed and rejoiced. Afterwards Evelyn must come and see the old Signora – the very old Signora now. At once the girl would go and tell her. The old Signora loved people to return.

'I was still a student,' Evelyn told her as she came with the soup, 'under twenty. Oh, it was wonderful to have free wine put on the table, just like a water-jug. We hardly drank wine in England then.'

'You speak beautiful Italian,' said the waitress. 'Students have been coming here and learning good Italian, the old Signora says, for a hundred years. When were you here? Ha!' (she clapped her hands) 'Then I was the baby in the kitchen. Now' (she stroked her stomach) 'soon there shall be another baby in the kitchen.'

'I'd like to be at the long table,' said Evelyn over the pasta, which seemed very plain.

'Nobody's sitting there.'

'Everyone used to sit there. All together. Like in *A Room with a View*. D'you think we could ask? Nobody's sitting there.'

'If nobody's sitting there we might as well stay over here by the window.'

'No – if we sat there, then other people would come. We could talk. Oh Mick – I wore such a dress. Tartan taffeta! Can you imagine? I thought you had to change for dinner, you see. I'd never been anywhere, just read Forster and Henry James. All the others were in beads and rags. It was the new fashion – rags. I hadn't met it. I was terribly behind the times.'

'This wasn't the time when you were with The Love of your Life?'

'No. I told you. It was just after Finals. Waiting for the results. I was with a girl who was chucking Medicine and going to be a nun. She went into a nunnery as soon as we got home. It was her last holiday.'

'Must have been a jolly little outing.'

'Mick'– Her laughter warmed him more than the eyewatering wine. He leaned across and took her hand. 'I'm glad you didn't go into a nunnery,' he said.

'Oh, I was pretty boring. I hadn't even got hooked on Medicine then. I only wanted everyday sort of things.'

The door of the dining room opened and an English family, mother, father and five children – filed in and sat at the long table. The older children folded their hands. The younger ones sat still and good. The youngest, a girl about seven, sat on her hands, her short arms stiff at each side of her until the father turned bleak wire spectacles on her and said 'Elizabeth.' Then she took her hands from under her thighs and folded them in her lap like the rest, but the corners of her mouth became very firm. She was unusually beautiful.

'What a beautiful child,' said Evelyn. Other people at side tables were looking too.

'Yes. Come on, love, what shall we have next?'

'No choice. It's a pensione. Osso bucco every night. I told you. Mick – just look at that child.'

'Yes. Let's have some more wine. Leave them be.'

'Why should I? I'm all right you know. You don't have to worry. For heaven's sake, look at them all. Aren't they beautiful?'

'The mother's not,' said Mick. 'She looks worn out.' 'Yes.' Evelyn looked vaguely, but then back at the children, especially at the child Elizabeth.

'What a father,' said Mick, seeing the glasses gleam from one child to another, then the order given for all to say Grace. Five pairs of eyes shut around him. Five pairs of hands were folded together. The wife moved spoons about the cloth.

' "For what we are about to receive," ' said the father –

'I don't believe it,' Mick said. 'They must be ghosts. I'll bet they're from Hampstead.'

The children began to drink soup which had been rather laconically slapped down by the young Signora. The child, Elizabeth, looked round as the young Signora pranced by and the young Signora tickled the top of the child's head. Again the father said, 'Elizabeth.' The mother continued to stare into space.

'Shall we go to bed now?' Evelyn was across the dining room almost before she had said it.

'Aren't we going out?' He hurried after her. 'For a walk? See the Duomo and all that? I think they floodlight it. It's too early to sleep.'

'No. You go and see it if you like. I'm tired. We'll be out all day after this – every day from tomorrow morning. When Rupert comes there'll be no cloister left untrod.' Her face had lengthened and her eyes looked tired.

In his bed across the room from her he said, 'You're not sorry we came? It's a busy place for a convalescence.' He was staring at their painted ceiling, shadowy with carved angels.

She said, 'I remember this ceiling. D'you know, I think we were in this same room. I wonder if – the girl who became a nun, goodness, I've forgotten her name – I wonder if she remembers this ceiling.'

'You're not sorry, Evelyn? It maybe has been a bit soon.'

'Don't be a fool. God – children have miscarriages these days. Abortions, abortions - you hear of nothing else. A clinical fact of life now. Unless you're a Catholic. Even Catholics aren't what they were. Catholic doctors now are doing abortions in Africa. In the famine places. It's a rational matter.'

They both thought of the abortion reform posters they had passed, slapped over ancient buildings – church walls, palazzos – and modern banks and municipal offices, on the way from the station.

'Not my line of business, thank goodness.'

'Well, no – nor mine.'

'You're not trying to persuade yourself,' he said, 'that this is the same? This was no choice for heaven's sake.'

After a time, as the old wooden room cooled and crackled in the early night she said, 'No.' Then, 'What do they mean – choice?'

Rupert's arrival was like a salt breeze. He bounced into the mahogany and plush entrance hall, arms astretch and talking before the young Signora had finished opening the inner door for him. He was fresh from Cyprus – the archetypal, unwed, ageless English academic, rich, Greece-loving, sexless – all passions channelled into deep concern for friends: the man you meet at college who turns up about every five years looking exactly the same and remembering every last thing about you and telling you nothing of himself. One's lynch-pin, one's strong rock. 'My dears – dears! Out. Out. Out we go at once before we're eaten by the aspidistras.' He wrapped Evelyn in his arms, gazed adoringly at the smiling young Signora over her shoulder and grabbed hold of touched Mick's arm. Like many men with secret lives he touched people often and bravely, hating it.

'What a place you've found. Is it real? I saw a troupe of little Nesbitts making for the Boboli Gardens with hoops and kites – a neurotic Mama and a father from the Iffley Road.

'We think Hampstead.'

'My dears – Oxford. They can only be Oxford. Mum is a lecturer in – let's see – Thermo-Dynamics and Pa is - Pa is ha! He is a Biologist. He reads Peter Rabbit at home and picks apart little pussy cats in the daytimes. He glares down microscopes at the death agonies of gnats. One day the children will all silently pack their bags and away to California. And Mama will take a tiny pistol out of her poche and shoot him through the head.'

'You know them, Rupert?'

The three of them were clattering down the pensione's stone stairs under the vaulted archway to the piazza.

'But dozens of them. Whole families of them.'

'Oxford rather than Cambridge?'

'Oh – masses more of them at Cambridge. Cousins and cousins. But in Cambridge, dears, they don't dress their children in Greenaway-yallery. It's filthy tee shirts and shaven heads. All reading Stendhal at six. Shall I tell you what happened to me last time I went to Cambridge?' He was sweeping them along the Via Servi. The crowds smiled at him, parting before him. 'Drinks,' he said, 'with a Fellow of Queen's. Sitting there talking (Coffee? Coffee? Let's stop here.) – oh, post-structuralism, Japanese realist fiction, usual stuff. Out from behind a sofa comes youngest child wearing nappies and smoking a cigarette.'

'Pot?' said Mick.

'No no no – Russian Sobranie. Twenties stuff.'

Evelyn was laughing. 'You made that up, Rupert.'

She sat back at the café table, looked at the small coffee cups, the glasses of water, the sugar lumps wrapped in paper decorated with little pictures of Raphael's Virgin and Child. She lifted her face to the sun.

'Come on Rupert, you did,' said Mick. 'These children were History Man children. University of E.A.'

'Certainly not, dear. History Man children have nothing to do with Oxford. Nowadays they're churchgoers –1662. Learning their Collect for the day. The parents toy with communities – not communes, communities. Firmly, firmly in their own beds most of the time. If not it's away to the confessional and deep discussions over an evening milk drink. All terribly sweet. The children terribly ugly.'

Evelyn became still. She watched the sugar lump as the coffee turned it amber. 'Those pensione children weren't ugly.'

Rupert began to talk of Giotto saints and San Miniato, all of which, he said, if they hurried they could see before lunch. Evelyn wondered what he and Mick had said when Mick had telephoned Cyprus last week to say that their holiday together was now going to be a convalescence. Rupert stood right outside this area of loss, outside all areas of marriage. On Rupert's part the conversation would have been no more than a quick exclamation of regret – then details of his time of arrival.

Yet, as the days passed, it seemed odd how skilful Rupert was being at making Evelyn smile, in directing her away from precipices. As Mick stood vague before the

Michelangelos, Rupert kept at Evelyn's side. While Mick made no plans, Rupert had pages marked each day in maps and guide books. It was Rupert who saw to it ('My dears, this is a holiday – not a *penance*') that they ate all their meals away from the pensione except for breakfast which they ate alone in their bedrooms. The admirable English family faded as if they had been the miasma they had looked.

On Rupert's last day, in the woods above Fiesole, they picniced and talked and sunbathed and slept and Evelyn awoke feeling brisk and well. In her old, incisive mood she talked of packing and, back in Florence, Rupert even allowed her to do some of this for him. He smiled at her with love as they all three struggled through the screaming rush-hour traffic to the railway station In one of the painted, horse-drawn carriages he had insisted upon.

'Dotty things,' said Evelyn. '*Sentimental*, Rupert.' When she had been here before they had been the only sort of taxi. It had been different then. Pretty. Romantic. But now they were going to miss the train. Times change. You have to face reality.

'Don't you, Rupert dear?'

'No,' said Rupert, kissing her, waving goodbye, scattering largesse to porters, leaping the train as it began to move out.

'Not all at once at any rate,' he called. 'Give it time. Let it face you.'

It was quiet without him that evening. They were tired and the pensione was dark and still and nearly empty. The long centre table was no longer made up and they sat in their alcove with only one old lady, bent like a leaf over her library book, at another. The food was a little less staid than on their first night, the wine kinder, the noise of the traffic less disturbing. There had been one of the frequent Florentine power cuts and the stately young Signora had placed a candle inside a bell of glass on each table so that shadows made the white-washed walls serene. Evelyn and Mick sat long over their coffee. The old lady closed her book and crept away.

Then the door opened and the English family, very slightly flushed in the face, swept steadily in like a river and sat down at the long table without a word. The young Signora coming through to remove the old lady's plate and blow out her candle, stopped and gasped. It was past nine o'clock. Over two hours late. It was as clear as if the Signora had shouted it that the kitchen was empty, the cook abed, the ovens cold. She said nothing, stood still, then after a pause went away and the family sat staring straight ahead. After quite a few minutes the Signora returned and asked, with a catch in her voice, whether they would take soup.

'Please,' said the father, candlelight on his glasses.

In the considerable time that then passed, the father said once, 'Is something wrong?' and nobody answered him.

Soup came. The Signora could manage no smile. She did not even look at the child, Elizabeth. She handed the basket of bread to each of them and, turning her big body about, disappeared through the door with head high. 'Shall we go?' said Mick to Evelyn, who was looking all the time at the child, but Evelyn said, 'No. No. Wait please.'

'Oh, Evelyn.'

'No, just wait a bit longer. Please.'

From the shadows of the centre table somebody suddenly said very high and clear, 'The soup is cold.' The mother pushed hers away.

'I think,' said the father, 'that it must nevertheless be drunk, don't you?'

Two or three of the children put down their spoons. Elizabeth went on with the soup until it was finished.

'Shall we all finish the soup?' asked the father slowly, turning his head about. The children one by one picked up their spoons again, getting the soup down somehow with the help of the hard bread. The mother turned sideways and looked at the floor.

'Come along now, Elizabeth, eat your bread.'

'I have drunk the soup,' said Elizabeth, 'but the bread is too hard.'

'Then we shall hope that you can eat it later, shall we not?'

Pasta came, freshly made, the Signora hot in the face. Evelyn and Mick asked for more coffee and the Signora, serving it, suddenly blazed her eyes at Evelyn and poured forth a whispered torrent of Italian with backward movements of the head at the centre table. Evelyn nodded but did not take her eyes from the child.

'We shall not take meat or fruit,' said the father, 'we shall go to bed. For what we have received Elizabeth?' She did not look up.

'You have not eaten the bread.'

'It's too hard. I drank the soup.'

'Come along. Eat the bread.'

She did not move.

'For what we have received the Lord make us truly thankful. Come along. We shall go. And Elizabeth shall stay here until she has eaten the bread.'

They went out, one of the older boys giving Elizabeth a push in the back with a friendly finger, but nobody else paid any attention, the mother leaving the room first without a glance. All their feet could be heard receding down the corridor, crackling like a forest fire, and doors were heard to close.

Suddenly, all the electricity in the pensione came on in a flood and the child was revealed like a prisoner under a search-light, all alone at the long table. She sat stalwartly, with small, round, folded arms, looking at her hands, her mouth dogged, the bread untouched on the tired cloth.

'Shall we go now?' asked Mick, loudly and cheerfully, coughing a little, squeaking back his chair.

'No. No. Not yet. I want some more coffee.'

'We can't have *more* coffee, it's much too late.'

The Signora came in again and stopped to see the child sitting alone in the glare. She turned astonished eyes on Evelyn and Mick and started towards the centre table, but the dark, fierce air hanging around the child made her shy.

'You – finito? Everyone now?'

The child did not answer.

'Could we have more coffee? I'm sorry – I know it's terribly late,' called Evelyn and looking back over her shoulder at the child all the way to the door, the Signora made for the kitchen again.

Mick began to hum and pace the floor a little. He looked out of the window where the colonnade of the Innocenti blazed patchily above the whirling lights of the cars. Above was the starry sky. Turning into the room again, he said, 'Hard old bread, isn't it?' and went and sat down by the child. 'Enjoying your holiday?' he said. 'Expect it's all a bit of a bore, isn't it? Churches and stuff. I expect you'd rather be at the sea.'

Then he put out his hand and let it stay for a moment above the child's head. He let it drop and began slowly to stroke her hair. She flung up her chin and pulled away as though she had been stung and simultaneously the door to the corridor opened and the father stood in the dining room. He said, 'What is this?'

'I was talking to your daughter.'

'I'm afraid my daughter is not allowed to talk to strangers.'

'Isn't it rather unwise then to let her sit alone, long after her bedtime, in a room with only strangers in it?'

'She knows how to behave. She knows that she has to stay there until she has eaten the bread.'

'That's your affair –'

'It is.'

'It's your affair, but suppose that the strangers had not been us? To leave a small child alone. Late at night. In a foreign restaurant.'

'Hardly a restaurant I think.'

'You treated it as a restaurant tonight. Over two hours late for dinner. Never a word of apology. The one and only waitress tired out. Pregnant. Behaving like lord and peasant – I'm sorry. I'm sorry, but my wife and I have been horrified. Disgusted. Disgusted with you. Never seen such idiocy. Quaint. Victorian play-acting. You need a psychiatrist – not fit to have children.'

'Are you an authority on children?'

'I – yes. I am a doctor. I know a lot about children.'

'And how many have you?'

'That's not the point. I see a child being studiously, insanely – '

'Shall we continue this outside?'

'By all means. If you will send this child at once to bed.'

'I shall consider it when we have talked. Outside the room if you please. I don't believe in discussions of this sort in front of children.'

'Very well.'

As the father swung out of the room and Mick swung after him, Evelyn saw in her husband's eyes the remote, terrible band of dismay she thought she had dreamt before. He was blind to her. She put her head in her hands and thought, 'I never knew. In all the years, I never asked. I never knew. I never thought of him.'

Lifting her face, she found that the little girl was looking at her with interest. The bread was still uneaten on the cloth. Her face was serious. She said to Evelyn, 'Don't cry. It doesn't matter.'

'I'm not. I wasn't –'

'It was a puncture. We got late. He's terribly ashamed. It's all right.'

'I – I just didn't –'

Tramping feet, loud voices were to be heard returning and the child, looking kindly still at Evelyn, sighed and picked up the bread in both fists.

'Oh no – oh no! Please don't,' cried Evelyn. 'Please let me have it – please. I'll hide it in my bag. 'She held out her arms. 'Throw it me. Throw it me.'

But Elizabeth, shocked, turned away. 'It's all *right*,' she said, and began to munch.

The two men as they returned, saw first this loyal munching, and then Evelyn in her corner, weeping at last.

Here are some of the questions you can ask yourself about this story, in order to analyse the language, ideas and structure:

1 At what point in the story do we realise that Evelyn has not accepted the loss of her baby?
2 What clues are there in the story to suggest that she hasn't?
3 What do we learn about male/female relationships in the story?
4 Make any comments that you can on the structure of the story – about where and how the story begins and ends, and any movements or actions in the story.
5 What is the narrative point of view in the story? Through whose eyes do we experience the feelings and events? Are there any changes? Give a few examples to make this clear.
6 Comment on Gardam's use of detail in the story, giving examples from the text.
7 How does Gardam express Evelyn's feelings in the last part of the story?
8 What are your responses to Evelyn during and at the end of the story?
9 How would you describe the mood and atmosphere of the story?
10 What function does Rupert have in the story?
11 In what ways does Gardam use Elizabeth and her family?

And here are some student responses to question 1; compare them to your own. These were the parts of the text identified by different students as the moment when they realised Evelyn had not accepted the loss:

- 'I'm fit now,' she said. 'A miscarriage isn't an illness. It's usual. A blessing. We know it.'
- That her miscarriage of a child was a blessing was a fact that he had levelly insisted upon since it happened, two weeks ago.
- She listened thoughtfully, with a careful, consulting-room expression, not looking at him.
- 'Yes. Let's have some more wine. Leave them be.'
- Her face had lengthened and her eyes looked tired.
- 'Don't be a fool. God – children have miscarriages these days. Abortions, abortions – you hear of nothing else. A clinical fact of life now. Unless you're a Catholic. Even Catholics aren't what they were. Catholic doctors now are doing abortions in Africa. In the famine places. It's a rational matter.'
- 'What do they mean – choice?'
- Yet, as the days passed, it seemed odd how skilful Rupert was being at making Evelyn smile, in directing her away from precipices.
- 'Not all at once at any rate,' he called. 'Give it time. Let it face you.'
- 'Shall we go?' said Mick to Evelyn, who was looking all the time at the child, but Evelyn said, 'No. No. Wait please.'
- 'Please let me have it – please. I'll hide it in my bag.' She held out her arms. 'Throw it me. Throw it me.'
- and then Evelyn in her corner, weeping at last.

Commentary

As you can see from the above choices, the students' responses varied from early on in the story to the very end. This demonstrates to us the ambiguity within the story, and the multiple interpretations possible. This is another way of addressing AO4.

> AO4: The ability to articulate independent opinions and judgements, informed by different interpretations of literary texts by other readers.
>
> ASSESSMENT OBJECTIVES

To consolidate this point, read the following dialogue between students who had read the story. They are responding to questions 2 and 3:

Catherine: I thought that Evelyn seemed reconciled to losing the baby and not being able to have more.

Sarah: But it's so soon after the miscarriage, and the baby was quite developed.

Daniel: Look how she notices babies everywhere.

Sarah: She's trying to be brave, trying to rationalise. But Rupert directs her away from 'precipices' and that suggests she could fall, she's in danger. I know it's a metaphor, but it sounds like she's on edge.

Catherine: She seems bright and sensible though.

Sarah: It says in the story: '*, and then Evelyn in her corner, weeping at last*'. She has held the sorrow back, all through the story.

Daniel: Isn't she afraid that Mick doesn't feel how she does?

Catherine: Mick seems OK though, he seems controlled.

Daniel: But not at the end. Evelyn has to realise how bad he felt about the baby too.

Sarah: That's why he gets so angry about Elizabeth. They both get really caught up with her.

Daniel: She is the child they can't have, isn't she?

Catherine: Even though she hardly speaks in the story. She seems to represent something to them both.

Daniel: They both want to feel that her father is cruel, and that he doesn't appreciate her. She is beautiful. They both notice that.

You can see from this discussion that listening to others' views is a good way of working your way into a text. It's important that you keep coming back to the text to support your ideas, however. What these students were doing was to exchange ideas, and to think about their own. They were trying to establish informed opinion, rather than giving instant responses. In this way they were responding to AO4. Notice that 'other readers' can include fellow students, although you should make every attempt to widen your critical reading.

Let's return to the short story and examine one of Gardam's narrative techniques. Look at Question 5 again (page 103). This question is directed at **structure**.

Structure is not an easy concept to grasp, and many students fall back on vague comments. But you need to be precise and detailed when you respond to a question which includes structure – in prose just as much as in poetry.

You can see that in the student discussion above, the students touched upon this aspect of the story. They commented on the changes in both Evelyn and Mick at the end of the story. What do we see them do in the story? What do they actually do? How is the ending different from the beginning? What progress has Evelyn made – mental or physical?

Commentary

As in many short stories, in one sense not a great deal has actually happened. The couple have been on holiday, spent time with a friend and become involved with a family in the pensione. But what is significant is what happens within the characters, what they learn about themselves and each other. Time does pass in this story, which is the duration of a holiday. Notice that Gardam starts off with the couple already in Italy, though she describes the journey there, briefly, and with a focus on the babies and young children the couple encountered. There is already a particular **focus** on this idea.

Gardam also tells us about the miscarriage, though she deals with the aftermath before she describes the event, via Evelyn's memories of it. Already you can see that the events of the story are not, in one sense, in chronological order. This is important, since by noticing this, you are showing a grasp of the way that the writer is shaping her material. Gardam also sets the story in a place where Evelyn had already visited twenty years earlier, bringing in the dimension of a younger Evelyn, untouched by more recent events.

One idea which you can apply to your own text, is what you would consider to be the turning point of the story. If you can identify this, you are again analysing structure, because you are looking at how the writer is organising her material.

It is possible, of course, to disagree about the exact moment of the turning point, and it need not be anything dramatically obtrusive. But somewhere in any short story or novel, there has to be a point at which we realise that there has been a change of some kind, and that something has happened in order to bring this about.

It is a mistake to think that all short stories rely on a twist in the tale, because very many of them don't. But if nothing at all happened, the reader would almost certainly feel that there was little point in reading the story.

In this story, what brings about the change is the arrival of the English family, but more than that what the family, and in particular Elizabeth, comes to mean to Evelyn, and as we discover, to Mick too. The incident at the end of the story where Elizabeth refuses to eat the bread brings out suppressed feelings in both Evelyn and Mick. The writer doesn't tell us why this happens, but she shows us, and the difference between **showing** and **telling** is a very significant part of the narrative methods of a writer. The showing will not be the same for all of us, since the way we respond to the story will to some extent depend on our own experiences.

The writer quite deliberately does not describe, tell us about, Evelyn's feelings about her miscarriage when she looks back. But her selection of detail such as the 'small limp arms', the 'whimpering and scratching of the dog at the bedroom door' and the silver birch tree all show us the extent of her feelings.

And this, of course, is part of the point of the story in that Evelyn and Mick try to be 'steady' and not to reveal their feelings. So, of course, the ending of the story when we see 'Evelyn in her corner, weeping at last' has all the more impact because of the restraint of what has gone before.

Now look again at Question 5: What is the narrative point of view in the story? Through whose eyes do we experience the feelings and events? Are there any changes? Give a few examples to make this clear.

It is important to be aware of the writer's use of a **narrative point of view**. Sometimes students assume that the first person point of view automatically evokes sympathy, and is the only way to get inside a character's head. But writing is more subtle than this.

Ask yourself one question: who did you think was the main character?

One comment that could be made about this story is that the reader obviously focuses on Evelyn, although the story is also about Mick.

Now a follow-up question: who speaks and who sees?

Asking yourself this question is a very good way of understanding the narrative point of view in a text. And it is one reason why it is too simple to assume that first person narrative is the only method of letting us know the thoughts and feelings of a particular character. For example, do any events take place in the story that we don't see through Evelyn's eyes?

I think you will agree that it is Evelyn's who sees, though since the story is written in the third person, it is not she who speaks. And sometimes, the narrator gives information about one character which no other character could be aware of.

Look back at this extract from the story:

> Rupert's arrival was like a salt breeze. He bounced into the mahogany and plush entrance hall, arms astretch and talking before the young Signora had finished opening the inner door for him. He was fresh from Cyprus – the archetypal, unwed, ageless English academic, rich, Greece-loving, sexless – all passions channelled into deep concern for friends: the man you meet at college who turns up about every five years looking exactly the same and remembering every last thing about you and telling you nothing of himself. One's lynch-pin, one's strong rock. 'My dears – dears! Out. Out. Out we go at once before we're eaten by the aspidistras.' He wrapped Evelyn in his arms, gazed adoringly at the smiling young Signora over her shoulder and grabbed hold of touched Mick's arm. Like many men with secret lives he touched people often and bravely, hating it.

Here, the narrator seems to be commenting on Rupert from a point of view that is not Elizabeth's. The reader is told what Elizabeth could not see, in the sense that no other character within the text could make this judgement. It requires a detached observer, a narrative voice that knows the secret lives of her character. It raises the issue of Rupert's role within the story. What function does he fulfil? For one thing, he is not Evelyn or Mick. This sounds obvious, but it is important. We need another character to enable us to understand more about the relationship of the central couple. Partly, Rupert makes us see that Evelyn is suffering, even though the story understates this deliberately. In the way that the story needs Elizabeth in order to expose the real pain of Evelyn and Mick, the story needs Rupert to give us a superficial change of mood, which also underlines Evelyn's sorrow and need for protection and distraction.

You can see from even a brief extract that the narrative point of view is flexible and not always easy to work out. But it is important to be aware of it, and its effects. You can see from this story that the reader can be positioned inside and outside a character. Look at this extract:

Here Gardam is using a technique known as **free indirect speech**. We move from inside to outside the character's head, in that at times we seem to be hearing her own words. To show you what this is, and how it works, look at these sentences from the story:

1 They had been married twelve years. **2** For fifteen she had been doing medical research, as busy as he in the same teaching hospital. **3** On her marriage she had made it clear that she had no intention of wasting herself – her youth, her training – in childbearing. **4** Her brain was at its best. **5** Children could come later. **6** Good heavens, you could have a child at forty now. **7** There was that top Civil Servant woman who had had a child – perfectly healthy child – at fifty. **8** It had always been so – able women often produced children late. **9** Mrs Browning – **10** (For Evelyn was properly educated: literary as well as medical.)

Are these the narrator's words or Evelyn's?

Here are my suggestions:

- Sentences 1 and 2, seem to be the narrator's words, so we are outside looking in.
- Sentence 3 is less straightforward though it does read like the narrator's comments on Evelyn's response to her situation.
- Sentence 4 – Evelyn's own voice.
- Sentence 5? – Probably Evelyn.
- In sentence 6 – We are inside Evelyn's head.
- In sentence 7 – We are inside Evelyn's head.
- Sentence 8 – Still Evelyn, though the tone is becoming more detached.
- Sentence 9 – A reference made by Evelyn to herself.
- Sentence 10 – Sounds like the narrator's judgement of her character.

From this analysis you can see how subtle and flexible the technique is. The writer enables the reader to make judgements about a character. We can simultaneously feel understanding of the character, but also can evaluate them. If this is combined with an analysis of language and dialogue, you as the reader, can demonstrate your awareness and understanding of the writer's narrative techniques, whilst using appropriate terminology. And you will avoid simplifications like assuming that only first person narrative evokes sympathy in the reader.

Dialogue in the story is used with variety and subtlety. For one thing, you might have noticed that there is a great deal that Evelyn and Mick don't say. Their exchanges tend to be limited: Rupert chatters much more freely. And there are times in the story when the writer deliberately doesn't say what passed between them:

> To conceive a child again must be out of the question.
> 'Why?'
> He told her.

We are given a sense that there is so much that has to be avoided, as if once they start to talk they will be afraid of what they might say. And because the focus of the story is Elizabeth, we see her become aware of the way that her understanding of Mick is limited:

Evelyn saw in her husband's eyes the remote, terrible band of dismay she thought she had dreamt before. He was blind to her. She put her head in her hands and thought, 'I never knew. In all the years, I never asked. I never knew. I never thought of him.'

The repetition here stresses her recognition. She had never thought of his pain, but of her own. These effects all work together in enabling you to analyse the methods of the writer, and explain what effects they have.

> **ASSESSMENT OBJECTIVES**
>
> If you can examine the language and techniques closely like this, you are responding to both AO1 and AO3, as well as implicitly to AO4.

5.3 Narrative voices

AQA A	U1
AQA B	U1
OCR	U2
WJEC	U2

Alice Walker's novel *The Color Purple* uses the **epistolary** form – that is, it is written in letters. This makes it possible for the reader to see changes in the life, attitudes and feelings of the narrator, Celie. We can see her developing confidence reflected in the letters she writes.

Here are two letters, one from the earlier part of the novel and one later. Which is which, and how can you tell?

Letter A

Dear Nettie,

The only piece of mail Mr. — ever put directly in to my hand is a telegram that come from the United States Department of Defense. It say the ship you and the children and your husband left Africa in was sunk by German mines off the coast of someplace call Gibralta. They think you all drowned. Plus, same day, all the letters I wrote to you over the years come back unopen.

I sit here in this big house by myself trying to sew, but what good is sewing gon do? What good is anything? Being alive begin to seem like a awful strain.

Your sister,

Celie

Letter B

Dear God,

Mr. — finally come right out an ast for Nettie hand in marriage. But He won't let her go. He say she too young, no experience. Say Mr. — got too many children already. Plus What about the scandal his wife cause when somebody kill her? And what about all this stuff he hear bout Shug Avery? What bout that?

I ast our new mammy bout Shug Avery. What it is? I ast. She don't know but she say she gon fine out.

She do more then that. She git a picture. The first one of a real person I ever seen. She say Mr. — was taking somethin out his billfold to show Pa an it fell out an slid under the table. Shug Avery was a woman. The most beautiful woman I ever saw. She more pretty then my mama. She bout ten thousand times more prettier then me. I see her there in furs. Her face rouge. Her hair like somethin tail. She grinning with her foot up on somebody motocar. Her eyes serious tho. Sad some.

I ast her to give me the picture. An all night long I stare at it. An now when I dream, I dream of Shug Avery. She be dress to kill, whirling an laughing.

Commentary

It isn't difficult to see that I have reversed the order of the extracts. Alice Walker is not trying to suggest that Black English is inferior to Standard English. Celie still retains features of her own kind of English. But if you set certain sentences side by side, you can see how the change in style reflects Celie's growing confidence.

Early letter (Letter B)	*Later letter (Letter A)*
I ast our new mammy bout Shug Avery	Plus, same day, all the letters I wrote to you over the years come back unopen.
An all night long I stare at it	I sit here in this big house by myself trying to sew, but what good is sewing gon do?
Sad some	Being alive begin to seem like a awful strain

If you look at these examples, you can see that Celie has developed the ability to write in longer and more complex sentences. She asks herself questions and thinks about her own feelings. She no longer accepts the world around her but is more aware of her own place in it.

You may well have noticed that she is writing a letter to a person, not to God, even though she thinks the addressee of the letter is no longer alive. But Celie no longer needs to address her letters to God, since she has real people in her life. She explained earlier that she wrote to God because there was no one else she could express her feelings to. Now her life has changed.

But by examining the way she writes, what you are doing is being more **analytical**, and not simply **describing** the content. You can also see that the **form** of this novel – the letters – is inescapably linked to what it is about.

Comparison

This is an extract from the first chapter of *Enduring Love* by Ian McEwan (1998). What is being described here is the attempt by four men, all strangers, to rescue an escaping hot air balloon, carrying a child. The narrator is Joe, a science writer. The crucial issue here is which of the four men let go of the ropes first.

> Mostly, we are good when it makes sense. A good society is one that makes sense of being good. Suddenly, hanging there below the basket, we were a bad society, we were disintegrating. Suddenly the sensible choice was to look out for yourself. The child was not my child, and I was not going to die for it. The moment I glimpsed a body fall away – but whose? – and I felt the balloon lurch upwards, the matter was settled; altruism had no place. Being good made no sense. I let go and fell, I reckon, about twelve feet. I landed heavily on my side and got away with a bruised thigh. Around me – before or after, I'm not so sure – bodies were thumping to the ground. Jed Parry was unhurt. Toby Greene broke his ankle. Lacey, the oldest, who had done his National Service with a paratroop regiment, did no more than wind himself.
>
> By the time I got to my feet the balloon was fifty yards away, and one man was still dangling by his rope. In John Logan, husband, father, doctor and mountain rescue worker, the flame of altruism must have burned a little stronger. It didn't need much. When four of us let go, the balloon, with six hundred pounds shed, must have surged upwards. A delay of one second would have been enough to close his options. When I stood up and saw him, he was a hundred feet up, and rising, just where the ground itself was falling. He wasn't struggling, he wasn't kicking or trying to claw his way up. He hung perfectly still along the line of the rope, all his energies concentrated in his weakening grip. He was already a tiny figure, almost black against the sky. There was no sight of the boy. The balloon and its basket lifted away and westwards, and the smaller Logan became, the more terrible it was, so terrible it was funny, it was a stunt, a joke, a cartoon, and a frightened laugh heaved out of my chest. For this was preposterous, the kind of thing that happened to Bugs Bunny, or Tom, or Jerry, and for an instant, I thought it wasn't true, and that only I could see right through the joke, and that my utter disbelief would set reality straight and see Dr Logan safely to the ground.

Possible question format

A question set by AQA B focuses on the part of the novel's first chapter which includes this sequence.

What we have is a novel told in the first person, although in a different way from *The Color Purple*. Joe is trying to make sense of, or justify, his own behaviour. Part of the AQA B question asks the candidate to write about the significance of the sequence of which this extract is a part. Candidates are directed to Joe's response to the events, and the way he describes them. As in many other similar questions, they are also directed to link this to the rest of the novel.

This is a common format for questions, which you need to be aware of.

What would you select from the extract above?

Some suggestions

The narrator is telling us of very dramatic events. For him, however, they raise ethical issues. How do we react when our life is at risk, and in this case at risk for an unknown child? If Celie in *The Color Purple* has to gain confidence in order to reflect, and question the world around her, Joe, it is clear, reflects on the significance of events constantly. The description is precise, and in some ways dispassionate, that is, not really emotionally involved. What seems to concern Joe is the moral rightness or wrongness of actions – the moral responsibility.

The question of who let go of the rope first is one that returns to him throughout the novel. The guilt that would arise if he felt that he let go first, and caused a man's death (as Dr Logan, inevitably, is killed), is a constant factor in the novel.

Another aspect that is **foregrounded** is the chance encounter of four men whose lives become linked because of this dramatic event. This is a link to the rest of the novel, when one of the men develops an obsessive interest in Joe.

A selection of words and phrases from the extract from this novel which show Joe's concern with **moral choices** – that is, how we decide what is right to do – could include:

- 'Mostly, we are good when it makes sense.'
- 'A good society is one that makes sense of being good.'
- 'we were a bad society, we were disintegrating'
- 'the sensible choice was to look out for yourself'
- 'altruism had no place'
- 'Being good made no sense.'
- 'the flame of altruism must have burned a little stronger'.

If you look at the phrases I have selected, you can see that they are taken mostly from the first part of the extract, and that they are very much concerned with 'good', 'bad' and 'sense'. 'Altruism' means unselfishness, acting for others and not for yourself.

When McEwan, via Joe, describes the plight of Dr Logan, we can see that Joe gives details of the incident: 'He was already a tiny figure, almost black against the sky.' It seems important to Joe that he recognises the reasons for what happens, and records accurately his own responses. He seems almost callous in his description of his feelings at the end of this extract. The idea that the sight of Dr Logan is 'so terrible it was funny, it was a stunt, a joke, a cartoon' may shock.

McEwan is showing us via Joe the honest responses of such a character, who analyses his own feelings and reactions. This fits in with the focus on 'good' or 'bad' actions in the earlier part of the extract. It also leads us in to the kind of preoccupations of the rest of the novel, when two kinds of looking at the world, Joe's and Jed Parry's, clash.

Progress check

You will need to refer closely to the text to respond to this kind of question, because it is not enough to describe what happens, you also need to work out how the writer is doing it. And you need to remember too, that first person narrative does not necessarily invite us always to sympathise with the speaker; it is always open to us to judge, and often the writer is encouraging us to do so.

Summary

If you think back to the characters in the texts we have discussed so far in this chapter you can see that the writer has different techniques available to him or her, and that you need to think very carefully about the text in order to decide what impact the techniques have. The **narrative voice** is crucial in the **presentation** of characters and relationships. Focus on how the writer achieves his or her effects rather than concentrating only on what you think the effects might be.

Further comparison

Look at the following extract from *The Handmaid's Tale* by Margaret Atwood (1985). In this novel, the narrator is Offred, a 'handmaid' whose job it is to give birth. The society she lives in is one in which women have been reduced to subordinate roles, and are allowed no real work or identity. Even Offred's real name is never known – she is of Fred, the name of her 'Commander', the man in charge of the household to which she has been posted in order to get pregnant, and the man who is meant to be the father of any child she can have. Reading and writing are forbidden to most members of this society, particularly the women who are allowed very little communication.

> I would like to believe this is a story I'm telling. I need to believe it. I must believe it. Those who can believe that such stories are only stories have a better chance.
>
> If it's a story I'm telling, then I have control over the ending.
>
> Then there will be an ending, to the story, and real life will come after it. I can pick up where I left off.
>
> It isn't a story I'm telling.
>
> It's also a story I'm telling, in my head, as I go along.
>
> Tell, rather than write, because I have nothing to write with and writing is in any case forbidden. But if it's a story, even in my head, I must be telling it to someone. You don't tell a story only to yourself. There's always someone else.
>
> Even when there is no one.
>
> A story is like a letter. *Dear You*, I'll say. Just you, without a name. Attaching a name attaches you to the world of fact, which is riskier, more hazardous: who knows what the chances are out there, of survival, yours? I will say you, *you*, like an old love song. You can mean more than one.
>
> You can mean thousands.
>
> I'm not in any immediate danger, I'll say to you.
>
> I'll pretend you can hear me.
>
> But it's no good, because I know you can't.

Commentary

What the writer does here is emphasise the importance of telling stories. We need to make sense of what happens to us. The ideas and issues in this novel are likely to appeal to many students since they concern a possible near future, and, of course, I am not suggesting that interest is wrong! However, as a student of English Literature, your focus should also be on the ways in which the writer chooses to tell the story.

Atwood chooses to focus on the **unreliability** of the narrator. She directs us to the fictional nature of the text. Offred talks about our need to communicate, to tell stories, to have a listener. In this society where open communication is denied, this is of even more significance. But in our own context, that of the reader of fiction, the effect is likely to be disturbing or unsettling. The end of the novel draws attention to the impossibility of real **closure**, as does this extract. Closure is a convention of fiction where all loose ends are tidied up, and everything is resolved. Atwood refuses to let us feel comfortable and safe, and therefore, your relationship, as reader, to the narrator of this novel will not be a comfortable one.

Her purpose as writer is not to reassure, and her narrative method is part of the way she fulfils her purposes.

KEY CONCEPTS

analysis	closure	describe
epistolary	foregrounding	form
moral choice	narrative voice	presentation

5.4 Significance of context

AQA A	U1
AQA B	U1
OCR	U2
WJEC	U2

Here are two extracts from *Knowledge of Angels* by Jill Paton Walsh (1994). The setting of this novel is an island in the Mediterranean, and the period, unspecified, but perhaps the fifteenth century. The island is disrupted by the appearance of two strangers: a wolf-child, and a castaway rescued from a shipwreck. Notice the ways in which the writer presents these characters to us.

Look at the differences between these two strangers.

[Extract A]

The *nevados* were three more days on the mountain, treading and cutting snow. They kept the wolf-girl tethered and staked on a leather thong. She refused their food and howled at night. When the time came to descend, they had trouble. The donkeys were terrified of her and refused to carry her, baring their teeth, and stubbornly resisting. She would not run on a lead, but would have needed to be dragged over every stone on the paths. When Luis tried to carry her, she bit his hand to the bone. They got her as far as the pine woods slung on a pole, bound wrist and ankle, like a carcass for the butcher, and stopped at the first band of trees to cut branches and make a cage. She seemed terrified of the cage and they had to beat her unconscious to get her into it. After that they took turns, carrying the cage on poles. Before they reached the first farms, Galceran had had enough of it. There would be no glory in having captured a child. He let Juan take her in exchange for the promise of a bottle apiece, and a basket of olives to share.

(Chapter 1)

[Extract B]

He had been in the water a long time. His skin was swollen, softened, pallid and wrinkled like the hands of their womenfolk on wash days. His lips were cracked. He was naked except for a sodden loincloth. Tumbled into the bottom of the boat he lay, eyes closed, face upwards, for a while. Then he groaned and rolled over and tried drinking the brackish slops in the bilge. They grounded the boat and carried the half-dead stranger up the beach. They laid him in the shade of the sailcloth tent and stared at him. He was a splendidly built man of middle age, bronzed-skinned and dark-haired, fully bearded. He reached for the water-flagon but they withheld it. Instead Lazaro dipped a sponge and held it to his lips, letting him suck and sip a little at a time. Miguel brought the oil jar – olive oil was plentiful on the island and they would have cooked their fishes in it at supper time – and rubbed oil into the waterlogged skin of the man's feet and hands. Then they pulled a closed sail over him and left him to sleep; his eyes were closed already in the utmost weariness.

(Chapter 2)

Commentary

This **presentation** is inextricably caught up with the setting of the novel. You can see that these two strangers are totally different, but one thing they have in common is their discovery by workers who have no real understanding of their significance.

Both of the characters are silenced and vulnerable, for different reasons. The wolf-girl is 'terrified' and her captors seem indifferent and brutal. They 'had to beat her unconscious' to get her into the cage. She is bound 'like a carcass for the butcher'.

The man in Extract B, on the other hand, is obviously wealthy and well-cared for. He is 'splendidly built', and his vitality in normal life is contrasted with his appearance now. He is 'bronzed-skinned and dark-haired, fully bearded', but having been in the water for days he is also 'half-dead', and the writer emphasises his physical state by words and phrases such as 'swollen, softened, pallid and wrinkled'. You can see how the men who find him think in terms of their ordinary lives: his skin is 'like the hands of their womenfolk on wash days'.

In a similar way, we can see that any sympathy for the plight of these two strangers is tempered by economic necessity. Olive oil can be given to the man, because 'olive oil was plentiful on the island', and they would have cooked their supper in it anyway.

And Galceran in Extract A exchanges the wolf-girl for 'the promise of a bottle apiece, and a basket of olives to share'. This is evidently the value they put on her life. There was 'no glory in having captured a child'.

Another way that you can look at these scenes is the disparity in the strangers – age, education, wealth, status, gender. If you think about this in conjunction with the setting, you can think about the ways in which the writer is setting up a situation in which there is room for all kinds of debate.

Clearly there is significance in the differences between the two outsiders, and the nature of the community itself. And, although the novel moves away from this setting, the rural beginnings of the novel prepare us for a possible clash of culture and ideas. We can see the setting as in some ways primitive, and this is followed up in the rest of the novel.

The writer has introduced us in this novel to a society alien to us, and then created two outsiders. There is a lot of potential for conflict of ideas, and plot development. The creation of the wolf-girl in particular has a great deal of **resonance**. By 'resonance' I mean an idea or feeling which has recurred over years, in different contexts, but always bringing with it some recognition, and many different associations. And the **juxtaposition** of the wolf-girl and the very different wealthy, but 'half-dead' stranger raises many questions and possibilities.

Progress check

It is always worth a close consideration of what the writer is setting up for us at the beginning of a text. Here are some points to bear in mind:

- Who is introduced first and in what context?
- What kind of society are we introduced to?
- Are there any obvious conflicts of character, setting, ideas, cultures, speech?
- Are there any obvious patterns or parallels to notice?
- What possible plot developments are there?

Comparison

Now compare the opening of *Snow Falling on Cedars* by David Guterson (1996).

> The accused man, Kabuo Miyamoto, sat proudly upright with a rigid grace, his palms placed softly on the defendant's table – the posture of a man who has detached himself insofar as this is possible at his own trial. Some in the gallery would later say that *his* stillness suggested a disdain for the proceedings; others felt it veiled a fear of the verdict that was to come. Whichever it was, Kabuo showed nothing – not even a flicker of the eyes. He was dressed in a white shirt worn buttoned to the throat and gray, neatly pressed trousers. His figure, especially the neck and shoulders, communicated the impression of irrefutable physical strength and of precise, even imperial bearing. Kabuo's features were smooth and angular; his hair had been cropped close to his skull in a manner that made its musculature prominent. In the face of the charge that had been leveled against him he sat with his dark eyes trained straight ahead and did not appear moved at all.

This is the actual opening paragraph of the novel. What questions does it raise? Here are my suggestions:

- Why is the man on trial?
- Why is his attitude like this?
- Is he guilty or innocent?
- How much longer after the trial is this story being told?
- Where is this set?
- What kind of society are we in?

Now select some of the words used to **present** this character. Here are some suggestions:

- 'proudly upright'
- 'rigid grace'
- 'a man who has detached himself'
- 'stillness'
- 'disdain'
- 'a fear'
- 'irrefutable physical strength and of precise, even imperial bearing'
- 'did not appear moved at all'.

When you pick out words and phrases in this way, it is possible to see the impact by gathering them together. The writer has combined description of this man's appearance with words which suggest his attitude and character. Words such as 'physical strength' and 'imperial bearing' combine with 'rigid' and 'proudly' to give an impression of immense self-control. One thing to notice is the **narrative voice**. The writer does not offer us a definitive view of the man, instead, he suggests what others think of him, and it is as if the writer himself can't know his own creation.

This does give an unusual effect, and reinforces the idea of a man who is enigmatic and mysterious. And this in turn makes it stranger that he is 'the accused man'. The writer is setting up for the reader many questions about the man and his situation.

ASSESSMENT OBJECTIVES

If you can pick out words in this way, and analyse their effects, you are showing your response to both AO3 and AO5i, as well as demonstrating your ability to **communicate the appropriate insight and terminology** (AO1).

Another kind of context

Sometimes writers choose subjects for their novels which are based on fact. Pat Barker's *Regeneration* (1991) is one example. This novel is based on the story of poet Siegfried Sassoon, and his encounter with W.H. Rivers, an army psychologist at Craiglockhart Hospital in 1917.

[Extract A]

Sassoon was trying to decipher a letter from H.G. Wells when Owen knocked on his door.

'As far as I can make out, he says he's coming to see Rivers.'

Owen looked suitably impressed. 'He must be really worried about you.'

'Oh, it's not *me* he wants to talk about, it's his new book.' Sassoon smiled.

'You don't know many writers, do you?'

'Not many.'

And I, thought Sassoon, am showing off. Which at least was better than moaning about Gordon's death to somebody who has more than enough problems of his own. 'I don't suppose he'll come. They all talk about it, but in the end it's just too far. I sometimes wonder whether that's why they put me here. Whether it was a case of being sent to Rivers or just sent as far away as possible.'

'Probably Rivers. He gets all the awkward ones.' Owen stopped in some confusion.

'Not that you're – '

'I count as awkward. By any standard.' He handed a sheet of paper across. 'For the *Hydra*.'

'May I read it?'

'That's the general idea.'

Owen read, folded the paper and nodded.

To forestall possible effusions, Sassoon said quickly, 'I'm not satisfied with the last three lines, but they'll have to do.'

[Extract B]

They ate in silence for a while. Rivers said, 'Have you heard from the friend you were going to write to about Gordon?'

'Yes. It's true apparently, he did die instantly. His father said he had, but they don't always tell parents the truth. I've written too many letters like that myself.'

'It must be some consolation to know he didn't suffer.'

Sassoon's expression hardened. 'I was glad to have it confirmed.' An awkward silence. 'I had some more bad news this morning. Do you remember me talking to you about Julian Dadd? Shot in the throat, two brothers killed? Well, his mental state has worsened apparently. He's in a – what I suppose I ought to call a mental hospital. Given present company. The awful thing is he's got some crazy idea he didn't do well enough. Nobody else thinks so, but apparently there's no arguing with him. He was one of my heroes, you know. I remember looking at him one evening. We'd just come in from inspecting the men's billets – which were lousy as usual, and – he cared. He really cared. And I looked at him and I thought, *I want to be like you.*' He laughed, mocking his hero-worship, but not disowning it. 'Anyway, I suppose I've succeeded, haven't I? Since we're both in the loony-bin.'

The provocation was deliberate. When Rivers didn't rise to it, Sassoon said, 'It makes it quite difficult to go on, you know. When things like this keep happening to people you know and and... love. To go on with the protest, I mean.'

Silence.

Sassoon leant forward. 'Wake *up*, Rivers. I thought you'd pounce on that.'

'Did you?'

A pause. 'No, I suppose not.'

Rivers dragged his hand down across his eyes. 'I don't feel much like pouncing.'

Commentary

In Extract A, Barker is using the meeting between Sassoon and the poet, Wilfred Owen. *Hydra* is the name of the magazine produced in Craiglockhart. They are talking about writing poetry. Barker is putting herself into the mind of a real person. What we have here is fiction that is quite deliberately using real people, places and events.

In Extract B, Barker writes about a meeting between Sassoon and Rivers in the Conservative Club.

Possible question format

Two kinds of questions

This text has been set by two exam boards, OCR and WJEC. The OCR question has as its focus the novel as a text, with reference to the extract in the **context** of the **whole text**, whilst WJEC focuses on the **context**, in terms of its **genre**.

The format of the OCR question is to 'consider the particular effects of this episode in the context of the novel as a whole'. WJEC asks the candidate to select an episode based on historical fact, and 'show how far your reading of *Regeneration* has been influenced by what is real and what is not'.

There are obviously different relevant definitions of context for you to bear in mind. The OCR question is more like the kinds of questions we have been discussing so far. However, the WJEC question is based on the novel as a piece of genre fiction. This particular genre – fiction based on fact – is now not unusual, and you might like to think about the effects created by using events from real life.

Here are some possible responses:

- the combination of real and imagined people
- the exploration of the effects of war
- an exposure and examination of a less well-known aspect of war
- an exploration of the psychology of war
- authenticity of voices, and perhaps feelings
- an ability to use our own knowledge of the First World War
- a widening of the scope of the subject matter of novels.

This weaving together of what is already known with what can only be imagined is an effective technique for a writer, and it would be hard to discuss this novel without seeing this as a key part of its impact.

You should never be afraid to make use of what you already know – the poetry of Sassoon and Owen, for example, in this case. The writer is aware that readers are coming to her book with prior knowledge, and it would be a pointless exercise to try to ignore this.

Summary

So, you can see that there are many kinds of context, and you should be ready to link this awareness with your understanding of the way texts work. And you should remember that texts themselves deal with contexts in terms of settings and relationships; often there is an exploration of the interaction between individuals and society, as well as between different characters.

If you do this, you are in effect meeting all of the assessment objectives.

KEY CONCEPTS

context	genre	juxtaposition
narrative voice	presentation	resonance

Sample question and model answer

Specimen question

Here is a question of a type set frequently on a prose text by all the boards.

> Refer to the beginning of *The Great Gatsby*. Discuss Fitzgerald's presentation of 'the valley of ashes', bringing out its significance in the novel as a whole.

The Great Gatsby

Chapter II

About half-way between West Egg and New York the motor road hastily joins the railroad and runs beside it for a quarter of a mile, so as to shrink away from a certain desolate area of land. This is a valley of ashes a fantastic farm where ashes grow like wheat into ridges and hills and grotesque gardens; where ashes take the forms of houses and chimneys and rising smoke and, finally, with a transcendent effort, of ash-grey men, who move dimly and already crumbling through the powdery air. Occasionally a line of grey cars crawls along an invisible track, gives out a ghastly creak, and comes to rest, and immediately the ash-grey men swarm up with leaden spades and stir up an impenetrable cloud, which screens their obscure operations from your sight.

But above the grey land and the spasms of bleak dust which drift endlessly over it, you perceive, after a moment, the eyes of Doctor T. J. Eckleburg. The eyes of Doctor T. J. Eckleburg are blue and gigantic – their retinas are one yard high. They look out of no face, but, instead, from a pair of enormous yellow spectacles which pass over a non-existent nose. Evidently some wild wag of an oculist set them there to fatten his practice in the borough of Queens, and then sank down himself into eternal blindness, or forgot them and moved away. But his eyes, dimmed a little by many pointless days, under sun and rain, brood on over the solemn dumping ground.

The valley of ashes is bounded on one side by a small foul river, and, when the drawbridge is up to let barges through, the passengers on waiting trains can stare at the dismal scene for as long as half an hour. There is always a halt there of at least a minute, and it was because of this that I first met Tom Buchanan's mistress.

In this case we will look at this section of the story only, but you can see from the format of the question how a part can be related to a whole.
Compare these two responses.

Answer A

Fitzgerald presents 'the valley of ashes' in a number of different ways. **1** The valley is not pleasant **2** and Fitzgerald makes it seem very grey. **3** He uses words like 'bleak' **4** and he keeps using the word 'grey'. **5** Even the river is 'foul', **6** and the scene is 'dismal'. **7** We don't get much sense of the narrator here, **8** instead this scene is very descriptive. **9** The eyes of Doctor Eckleburg dominate the scene as they are 'blue and gigantic' **10** though they 'brood' over the 'solemn dumping ground'. **11**

1 too general
2 well, no!
3 describing here, not analysing
4 still describing
5 yes, but to what effect?
6 still describing
7 still describing
8 don't we? And how is this significant?
9 ugh! Avoid this at all costs. And where is the answer going?
10 and what is the significance of this?
11 now we are listing bits of the text.

Answer B

Fitzgerald conveys the desolation of the valley by his use of language. **1** He uses the word 'grey' several times, building on the effect each time. **2** He compares the valley to 'a fantastic farm' emphasising its barrenness and its grotesque nature. **3** The ashes simulate life – people, landscape and gardens, but everything is lifeless in the extreme. **4** He stresses the impenetrability of the grey clouds, then links this to the eyes of Doctor T.J. Eckleburg. **5** The 'spasms of bleak dust drift endlessly' over the 'grey land', and the even the 'gigantic' eyes are 'dimmed', all suggesting ugly pointlessness. **6** The bizarre sight of the spectacles brooding over the 'solemn dumping ground' makes the scene even uglier. **7** Together they suggest a life that is dry and barren. **8** Even the oculist might have sunk down himself 'into eternal blindness' **9**

1 'desolation locates this for us a little more
2 trying to examine effects
3 the comment is developed and supported
4 further development
5 and more support – points linked, and related to text
6 comment on choice of language
7 development
8 pulling things together
9 extending the reference, and developing the argument
10 technical term correctly used

Sample question and model answer (continued)

11 the argument is sustained, and analysis shown. Reference to narrative voice, and use of critical terminology.

emphasising the lack of sight which is symbolic rather than literal. **10** at the end of this descriptive passage, we are reminded of Nick, the narrator who associates this bleak scene with Tom Buchanan and his mistress, already giving this relationship these same connotations of bleakness, barrenness, ugliness, and lack of sight. **11**

Even in two such short extracts from student answers, we can see great and significant difference between the quality of the responses. The margin notes should show you why the second answer would achieve a much higher grade than the first. The tendency of the first candidate is to describe rather than analyse. There is little comment on the presentation, and potentially interesting comments are then left. The second candidate, however, focuses on the methods of the writer, seems secure with terminology, and explores the effects of choice of language. Links are made and supported, and there is a real argument happening.

LEARNING SUMMARY

Jane Gardam's short story *'An Unknown Child'* was the focus of the first part of this chapter, with a stress on her narrative techniques and effects. Student answers were analysed in order to show what a focus on 'presentation' can be achieved, and there was further consolidation of key concepts.

The assessment objectives were foregrounded, and there was consideration of various set texts, all with the purpose of showing you how to analyse and explain writers' techniques and their effects. We looked at different ways of defining **context** including that of the societies in which novels are set, as well as different historical periods.

Exam practice and analysis

Question

This is an example of how a question might be divided up into different parts.

Enduring Love: Ian McEwan

Look again at Chapter 11 of the novel. Then respond to the following tasks.

(i) What does this letter reveal of Jed's character?

(ii) Comment on the position of this letter in relation to Chapters 10 and 12.

(iii) Although some readers sympathise with Jed Parry because of his illness, others find him a disturbing presence. How do you respond to him?

Notes

The different parts of the question are intended to target different objectives.

Part (i) examines your knowledge of the text, and ability to select relevant material (AO2i). Part (ii) looks specifically at structure (AO3). Part (iii) is directed to both AO4 and AOSi, inviting you to explore different interpretations, and arrive at your own.

Chapter 6

Drama

After studying this chapter you should know about:

LEARNING OBJECTIVES

- *effects of genre*
- *dramatic techniques: movement, dialogue, voices, conflict, tension*
- *skills: analysis; understanding of form and structure; asking the right questions; right and wrong approaches*

6.1 Assessment

AQA A U3
AQA B U2
EDEXCEL U1
OCR U3
WJEC U2
NICCEA U1

These are the drama texts set by the different boards, and the assessment objectives targeted:

AQA A

AOs 1: 5%; 2i: 5%; 3: 5%; 4: 10%; 5i: 5% Open Book

Richard Brinsley Sheridan: *The School for Scandal*
Arthur Miller: *All My Sons*
Oscar Wilde: *A Woman of No Importance*
John Ford: *'Tis Pity She's a Whore*
Brian Friel: *Making History*
Trevor Griffiths: *Comedians*

AQA B

AOs 1: 5%; 2i: 5%; 3: 5%; 5i 5% Closed Book

Arthur Miller: *Death of a Salesman*
Tennessee Williams: *Cat on a Hot Tin Roof*
Tom Stoppard: *Rosencrantz and Guildenstern Are Dead*
Caryl Churchill: *Top Girls*
Peter Shaffer: *Amadeus*
John Osborne: *Look Back in Anger*

EDEXCEL

AOs 1: 5%; 2i: 5%; 3: 5%; 4: 5% Open Book

Aphra Behn: *The Rover*
Brian Friel: *Translations*
Tennessee Williams: *A Streetcar Named Desire*
Caryl Churchill: *Top Girls*
Tom Stoppard: *Professional Foul*

OCR

No specified drama texts

WJEC

AOs 1: 5%; 3: 5%; 4: 20%

Brian Friel: *Translations*
Arthur Miller: *Death of a Salesman*

NICCEA

AOs 2i: 10%; 3: 10%; 4: 10%; 5: 10%

Robert Bolt: *A Man for all Seasons*
Brian Friel: *Making History*
David Mamet: *Glengarry Glen Ross*
Frank McGuinness: *Observe the Sons of Ulster Marching Towards the Somme*
Harold Pinter: *Betrayal*
Peter Shaffer: *Amadeus*
Tennessee Williams: *A Streetcar Named Desire*

ASSESSMENT OBJECTIVES

We will be using several of the above texts in order to explore the techniques needed to achieve the assessment objectives. You should bear in mind, though, that even if the texts discussed are not ones you are actually studying, the comments made are intended to apply to all the twentieth-century drama texts you are studying, for coursework as well as exam.

6.2 Genre

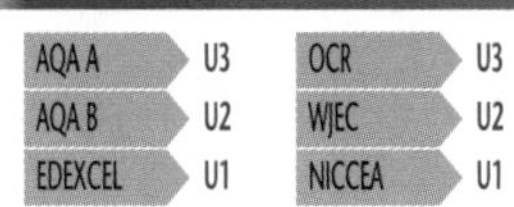

It is always important to bear in mind the **genre** of the text you are studying. This is particularly so in the case of drama, mainly because so many students tend to write as if a play were a novel set out rather oddly! Bear in mind that plays are written to be performed. You need to consider the movements and groupings on stage, not just the words, and the 'characters'.

In order to demonstrate this to you, look at the following extract from *The Devil's Disciple* by Bernard Shaw (1900). Richard Dudgeon, the estranged son, is returning to his family after a long absence. The play is set in America in 1777, and Richard's family are Puritans.

He is certainly the best-looking member of the family; but his expression is reckless and sardonic, his manner defiant and satirical his dress picturesquely careless. Only, his forehead and mouth betray an extraordinary steadfastness; and his eyes are the eyes of a fanatic.

Look at all Richard's actions.

RICHARD (*on the threshold, taking off his hat*) Ladies and gentlemen: your servant, your very humble servant. (***With this comprehensive insult, he throws his hat to Christy with a suddenness that makes him jump like a negligent wicket keeper, and comes into the middle of the room, where he turns and deliberately surveys the company.***) How happy you all look! how glad to see me! (***He turns towards Mrs Dudgeon's chair; and his lip rolls up horribly from his dog tooth as he meets her look of undisguised hatred.***) Well, mother, keeping up appearances as usual? That's right, that's right. (***Judith moves away from his neighborhood to the other side of the kitchen holding her skirt instinctively as if to save it from contamination. Uncle Titus promptly marks his approval of her action by rising from the sofa, and placing a chair for her to sit down upon.***) What! Uncle William! I haven't seen you since you gave up drinking. (***Poor Uncle William, shamed, would protest; but Richard claps him on his shoulder, adding***) You have given it up, haven't you? (***releasing him with a playful push***) Of course you have: quite right too: you overdid it. (***He turns away from Uncle William and makes for the sofa.***) And now, where is that upright horsedealer Uncle Titus? Uncle Titus: come forth. (***He comes upon him holding the chair as Judith sits down.***) As usual, looking after the ladies!

See how others respond.

UNCLE TITUS (*indignantly*) Be ashamed of yourself, sir–

His attitude to his family?

RICHARD (***interrupting him and shaking his hand in spite of himself***) I am: I am: but I am proud of my uncle – proud of all my relatives (***surveying them***) who could look at them and not be proud and joyful? (***Uncle Titus, overborne, resumes his seat on the sofa.***)

Look at the way Shaw handles the stage movements. In a way what Shaw does is unusual, as he writes long and complex stage directions. Sometimes, these include detailed comments about the appearance of his characters, almost as if they were in a novel, but at other times, he focuses on their actions, and the **dynamics** on stage. By 'dynamics' I mean the interactions of the characters on stage, and the ways they influence one another. The first part of the extract describes Richard's appearance in a way which makes clear the kind of character he is, but the **dialogue** and **stage directions** which follow reinforce this impression.

Student responses

One student made this comment on the above extract:

> It seems to me that Richard is like the ringmaster in a circus. He dominates the action all the time. Everyone reacts to him, although no one likes him. He does most of the speaking, and interrupts other characters. He moves about a lot, and makes the other characters seem almost paralysed by him. Uncle Titus moves, but Richard mocks his actions, so we are left in no doubt about who is in charge.

By making such a comment, she is showing that she has understood the generic nature of the text: that it is a play, and that it is meant to be performed.

Can you see the difference between a comment like the one above and this one, also by a student?

Richard is described as having 'the eyes of a fanatic'. The other characters obviously don't like him, but he does not seem to care. Uncle William is 'shamed', and Uncle Titus 'overborne'.

What the second student says is not wrong, and there is some textual support. What the comment lacks is some awareness that this is a play, and that movement is part of what the writer is saying. There is no real attempt to analyse the dynamics of the scene, as shown by their interactions both in speech and in actions.

Actions

Look now at a list of Richard's actions, taken from the stage directions in the extract. He:

- throws his hat
- comes into the middle of the room
- turns and deliberately surveys the company
- turns towards Mrs Dudgeon's chair
- claps him on his shoulder
- releasing him with a playful push
- interrupting him and shaking his hand.

Look at this question on *The Devil's Disciple*, based on the format of Edexcel questions, and you can tell how the above comments are relevant to AS answers.

Possible question format

Turn to Act 1, and remind yourself of the contents from the entrance of Richard Dudgeon until the stage directions '(*Uncle Titus, overborne, resumes his seat on the sofa*)'.

How effective do you find this scene dramatically in the context of the play as a whole?

Commentary

A key word here is 'dramatically'. You must pay close attention to the way that the scene is meant to be enacted on stage. But you also need to bear in mind the ways in which you can examine a scene in terms of its dramatic effectiveness in the whole text.

For example, think about the following:

- conflict
- movement
- pace
- changes
- revelations
- contrasts
- tension.

If you apply this to the extract above, you can see an obvious **conflict** between Richard and his family. Conflict is, of course, the mainspring of drama. A play in which everyone agreed about everything would undoubtedly leave the audience dissatisfied! Remember, though, that conflict can be internal as well as external. All of Shakespeare's tragic heroes are given soliloquies in which they express their inward conflict, for example, deciding on the rightness or wrongness of a course of action.

Richard's **movements** around the stage are noticeable. This is the way he dominates the action. And he moves quickly, giving the audience a sense of great **pace**, with sudden **changes** of both movement and speech. He obviously is aware of family secrets or **revelations** as he jokes about his uncle's vices. His appearance, language and behaviour form a definite **contrast** to the rest of the characters. The **tension** here between Richard and the rest of his family is obvious.

We can tie this in to the rest of the play, since this is an extract from early in the text. It seems clear that the play hinges on Richard's behaviour in contrast to the people around him. We can see that the play will concern itself with the unfolding of Richard's character, and the conflict with his family is obviously crucial. So, to answer the above question, what you will need to do is examine the importance of this, the first appearance of Richard. Thus we return to the points made previously about his dramatically effective entrance.

change	conflict	contrast	dialogue
dynamics	genre	movement	pace
revelation	stage directions	tension	

KEY CONCEPTS

6.3 Conflict and tension

AQA A	U2
AQA B	U2
EDEXCEL	U1
OCR	U3
WJEC	U2
NICCEA	U1

The stage directions which follow are taken from *A Streetcar Named Desire* by Tennessee Williams (1947). The play depends on a depiction of inner tension in the character of Blanche Dubois, an ageing American woman, who is aware of the secrets in her past which she is afraid will be revealed.

Look at the effect of Blanche's posture and movements.

BLANCHE *sits in a chair very stiffly with her shoulders slightly hunched and her legs pressed close together and her hands tightly clutching her purse as if she were quite cold. After a while the blind look goes out of her eyes and she begins to look slowly around. A cat screeches. She catches her breath with a startled gesture. Suddenly she notices something in a half opened closet. She springs up and crosses to it, and removes a whisky bottle. She pours a half tumbler of whisky and tosses it down. She carefully replaces the* bottle *and washes out the tumbler at the sink. Then she resumes her seat in front of the table.*

(Scene One)

You can see from these early stage directions that Blanche drinks secretly and desperately, and indeed desperation is associated with Blanche throughout the play as her secrets come into the light.

Light itself is an important **symbol** in the play. Blanche fears the light, and it comes to represent the ageing process, as well as the idea of truth being revealed. At one point, Blanche says: 'Turn that off! I won't be looked at in that merciless glare!' Towards the end of the play, Williams gives us this stage direction:

Tremblingly, she lifts the hand mirror for a closer inspection. She catches her breath and slams the mirror face down with such violence that the glass cracks. She moans a little and attempts to rise.

(Scene 10)

Notice that he is conveying her feelings by actions, not words. The fact that she is afraid of ageing is conveyed dramatically to the audience in this way. And look at these stage directions too:

What effect is Williams trying to convey?

The Poker Night. There is a picture of Van Gogh's of a billiard-parlour at night. The kitchen now suggests that sort of lurid nocturnal brilliance, the raw colours of childhood's spectrum. Over the yellow linoleum of the kitchen table hangs an electric bulb with a vivid green glass shade. The pokerplayers – **STANLEY, STEVE, MITCH** *and* **PABLO** *wear coloured shirts, solid blue, a purple, a red-and-white check, a light green, and they are men at the peak of their physical manhood, as coarse and direct and powerful as the primary colours. There are vivid slices of watermelon on the table, whisky bottles and glasses. The bedroom is relatively dim with only the light that spills between the portieres and through the wide window on the street. For a moment there is absorbed silence as a hand is dealt.*

(Scene 3)

Williams wants to show the contrast between Blanche who wears white, lacy clothes, and is compared to a 'moth' at various times in the play and the rougher, more aggressive world of the men in their 'primary colours'. Words such as 'lurid nocturnal brilliance', 'raw' and 'vivid' link with the clothes worn by the men which demonstrate their 'coarse', 'direct and powerful' qualities. You will notice that these stage directions, like some of those written by Shaw, include almost novelist-like descriptions. Williams is showing us a clash between two kinds of lives, and you can see from the above that the suggestion is that Blanche is bound to be the loser. She is associated with a kind of fading away, a refusal to accept reality.

At the same time, though, as his words indicate, we are not necessarily going to sympathise with the men, particularly Stanley, Blanche's brother-in-law, whose qualities are 'coarse' and crude, even if vital and 'direct'.

Williams also uses music dramatically. Blanche is associated with different kinds of music. Look at these examples:

> *The music of the polka rises up, faint in the distance.*
>
> (Scene 1)
>
> STANLEY *enters the kitchen from outside, leaving the door open on the perpetual 'blue piano' around the corner.*
>
> (Scene 2)
>
> BLANCHE *opens her eyes. The 'blue piano' sounds louder.*
>
> (Scene 3)
>
> STELLA *has embraced him with both arms, fiercely, and full in the view of* BLANCHE. *He laughs and clasps her head to him. Over her head he grins through the curtains at* BLANCHE. *As the lights fade away, with a lingering brightness on their embrace, the music of the 'blue piano' and trumpet and drums is heard.*
>
> (Scene 4)
>
> STELLA (*quietly*) Take me to the hospital.
>
> *He is with her now, supporting her with his arm, murmuring indistinguishably as they go outside. The 'Varsouviana' is heard, its music rising with sinister rapidity as the bathroom door opens slightly.* BLANCHE *comes out twisting a washcloth. She begins to whisper the words as the light fades slowly.*
>
> (Scene 8)
>
> *The luxurious sobbing, the sensual murmur fade away under the swelling music of the 'blue piano' and the muted trumpet.*
>
> (Scene 10)

As you can see from these examples covering the whole of the play, Williams is using a wide range of dramatic effects. And he uses them so that an impact is built up by **repetition**. We associate Blanche, and other characters, with certain recurring effects and symbols. The 'blue piano', for example, is bound to carry with it connotations of the melancholy mood we associate with that kind of music. At other times, music is louder and shriller, echoing Blanche's state of mind.

If you look back at the extracts from the play, you can see that what we have not done is examine the effects of dialogue. The focus has been on **dramatic effects** – those available only to the writers of plays. Therefore, we have concentrated on features of this **genre**. It's important that you always remember the different methods available to writers in different genres, and that you are able to support your answer by close reference to the text, as demonstrated above.

Other kinds of conflict

The focus in the last section was on inner conflict, and the ways the dramatist can reveal it to the audience. In contrast, we will now explore the ways in which a dramatist presents the conflict in a whole society, making political as well as personal statements. The play *Translations* by Brian Friel (1981) examines the effects of an Ordnance Survey mapping, and renaming of the local Gaelic place names. The setting is County Donegal in Ireland in 1833.

This is an extract from Act Two, Scene One. Owen is the son of Hugh, the local Hedge School master, and the brother of Manus. He has lived away from home in Dublin, leaving Manus to look after his drunken father. Lieutenant Yolland is in charge of the re-naming of the place names. Captain Lancey is his superior. Owen has been working for the Royal Engineers, the English who are doing the mapping, as a translator. The English soldiers refer to Owen as 'Roland'. Yolland has become increasingly sympathetic to the locals during his stay in Ireland.

OWEN What is happening?

YOLLAND I'm not sure. But I'm concerned about my part in it. It's an eviction of sorts.

OWEN We're making a six-inch map of the country. Is there something sinister in that?

YOLLAND Not in ...

Look at the ways the language reflects different attitudes.

OWEN ... And we're taking place-names that are riddled with confusion and ...

YOLLAND Who's confused? Are the people confused?

OWEN and we're standardising those names as accurately and as sensitively as we can.

YOLLAND Something is being eroded.

OWEN Back to the romance again. Alright! Fine! Fine! Look where we've got to. (***He drops on his hands and knees and stabs a finger at the map.***) We've come to this crossroads. Come here and look at it, man! Look at it! And we call that crossroads Tobair Vree. And why do we call it Tobair Vree? I'll tell you why. Tobair means a well. But what does Vree mean? It's a corruption of Brian – (***Gaelic pronunciation.***) Brian – an erosion of Tobair Bhriain. Because a hundred-and-fifty years ago there used to be a well there, not at the crossroads, mind you – that would be too simple – but in a field close to the crossroads. And an old man called Brian, whose face was disfigured by an enormous growth, got it into his head that the water well was blessed; and every day for seven months he went there and bathed his face in it. But the growth didn't go away; and one morning Brian was found drowned in that well. And ever since that crossroads is known as Tobair Vree – even though that well has long since dried up. I know the story because my grandfather told it me. But ask Doalty – or Maire – or Bridget – even my father – even Manus – why it's called Tobair Vree; and do you think they'll know? I know they don't know. So the question I put to you, Lieutenant, is this: What do we do with a name like that? Do we scrap Tobair Vree altogether and call it – what? – The Cross? Crossroads? Or do we keep piety with a man long dead, long forgotten, his name 'eroded' beyond recognition, whose trivial story nobody in the parish remembers?

Why such a long speech?

YOLLAND Except you.

OWEN I've left here.

YOLLAND You remember it.

OWEN I'm asking you: what do we write in the Name-Book?

YOLLAND Tobair Vree.

Look at the contrasting short lines of dialogue in the rest of the extract.

OWEN Even though the well is a hundred yards from the actual crossroads – and there's no well anyway – and what the hell does Vree mean?

YOLLAND Tobair Vree.

OWEN That's what you want?

YOLLAND Yes.

OWEN You're certain?

YOLLAND Yes.

OWEN Fine. Fine. That's what you'll get.

YOLLAND That's what you want, too, Roland.

(***Pause***)

OWEN (***Explodes***) George! For God's sake! My name is not Roland!
YOLLAND What?
OWEN (***Softly***) My name is Owen.
(***Pause***)
YOLLAND Not Roland?
OWEN Owen.
YOLLAND You mean to say –?
OWEN Owen.
YOLLAND But I've been –
OWEN O-W-E-N.
YOLLAND Where did Roland come from?
OWEN I don't know.
YOLLAND It was never Roland?
OWEN Never.
YOLLAND O My God!
(***Pause. They stare at one another. Then the absurdity of the situation strikes them suddenly. They explode with laughter.*** **OWEN** ***pours drinks.***)

So, what mood have we ended with?

Commentary

You can see that what Friel is doing is presenting dramatically the effects of a clash of cultures, not just a personal conflict. But he needs to **embody** the cultural differences for the audience. A play that was solely concerned with ideas would probably hold very little interest for an **audience**, and it is vital that in your discussion of drama you always think about the effects on those who are watching.

In this extract the focus is on the **cultural** importance of place names. But the debate is not a dry or dull one because the two men show us different attitudes. And it is the Englishman, the soldier Yolland, who is most sympathetic to the idea of retaining the place name 'Tobair Vree', whilst Owen is more dismissive.

Possible question format

Here is a question on this text modelled on questions from Edexcel.

Remind yourself of Act 2, scene 1 and consider in detail the ways in which Friel reveals the importance of language here and in at least one more scene.

Commentary

Think here about the way the extract reveals the significance of names. The focus is on re-naming – firstly of a place name 'Tobair Vree' and then of Owen himself. What do you think Friel is saying about the importance of names?

Here are two ideas:

- Names equate with identity.
- When a name is lost its history is lost with it.

What words does Yolland use that suggest loss? The words 'eviction' and 'eroded' are used whilst as far as Owen is concerned the operation is to 'standardise' names because the people are 'confused'. We can see through the dialogue between the two men that Friel is showing that language is weighted with significance. Owen has separated himself from his home and family and returned as a translator. He is eager to modernise, to bring his homeland out of the past: he has, after all, been living in the city. Yet Owen is aware of the history of the name 'Tobair Vree'.

When a name disappears, all that has led to that name goes too, inevitably. In the play as a whole, language and communication are crucial. The English soldiers, seen by the locals as 'colonialists', do not know the Irish language, though Yolland wants to learn it as he becomes more aware of the local people and their culture.

But it is not enough to identify the issues. Friel is making them **dramatic**. We need to see the issues in terms of two men from different backgrounds, each of whom is changing and being changed. We can see that Owen has tolerated being called Roland, but his increasing friendship with Yolland leads him to 'explode' that his name is not Roland. These characters react to one another. They are in a relationship which relies on communication and language, though at the same time Friel makes it clear to the audience that the role of the English in Ireland makes lasting friendships between the Irish and the English intruders impossible.

Therefore, what we see in this scene is both personal and political. And the obstacles as well as the communication depend upon language.

KEY CONCEPTS

audience	culture	drama
dramatic effects	embodiment	genre
repetition	symbol	

6.4 Voices

AQA A	U3
AQA B	U2
EDEXCEL	U1
OCR	U3
WJEC	U2
NICCEA	U1

When discussing prose, we looked at the importance of the narrative voice and the narrative point of view. In drama, voices are all we have – voices and the directions from the writer about the way the dialogue should be spoken, and any actions that accompany it, as well as the stage setting.

In order to analyse the effects of voices in plays, we will now look at a number of extracts, all taken from set texts.

Extract A

The first extract is from *Educating Rita*, by Willy Russell (1985). Rita, a hairdresser, has come for tuition for her Open University course to Frank, a lecturer at a university. The play consists only of these two characters.

RITA Is that because of me, because of what I said last week?

FRANK (*laughing*) My God. You think you've reformed me?

RITA (*going to the window*) I don't wanna reform y'. Y' can do what y' like. (*Quickly*) I love that lawn down there. When it's summer do they sit on it?

FRANK (*going to the window*) Who?

RITA (*going back to the desk*) The ones who come here all the time. The proper students.

FRANK Yes. First glimmer of sun and they're all out there.

RITA Readin' an' studyin'?

FRANK Reading and studying? What do you think they are, human? Proper students don't read and study.

RITA Y' what?

FRANK A joke, a joke. Yes. They read and study, sometimes. (*Pause.* **RITA** *dumps her bag on the chair and then goes and hangs up her coat on the door.*)

RITA It looks the way I always imagined a public school to look, y' know a boardin' school. When I was a kid I always wanted to go to a boardin' school.

FRANK God forbid it; why?

RITA (*going to her chair at the desk*) I always thought they sounded great, schools like that, y' know with a tuck-shop an' a matron an' prep. An' a pair of kids called Jones minor an' Jones major. I told me mother once. (***She opens her bag and takes out the copy of 'Howards End', ring-bound file, note-pad, ruler and pencil-case, placing them methodically on the desk in front of her.***) She said I was off me cake.

FRANK (***with an exaggerated look at her***) What in the name of God is being off one's cake?

RITA Soft. Y' know, mental.

FRANK Aha. I must remember that. The next student to ask me if Isabel Archer was guilty of protestant masochism shall be told that one is obviously very off one's cake!

RITA Don't be soft. You can't say that.

FRANK Why ever not?

RITA You can't. If you do it, it's slummin' it. Comin' from you it'd sound dead affected, wouldn't it?

FRANK Dead affected?

RITA Yeh. You say that to your proper students they'll think you're off your – y' know ...

FRANK Cake, yes. Erm – Rita, why didn't you ever become what you call a proper student?

RITA What? After goin' to the school I went to?

FRANK Was it bad?

(RITA ***starts sharpening the pencils one by one into perfect spikes, leaving the shavings on the desk.***)

RITA Nah, just normal, y' know; borin', ripped-up books, broken glass everywhere, knives an' fights. An' that was just in the staffroom. Nah, they tried their best I suppose, always tellin' us we stood more of a chance if we studied. But studyin' was just for the whimps, wasn't it? See, if I'd started takin' school seriously I would have had to become different from me mates, an' that's not allowed.

FRANK By whom?

RITA By your mates, by your family, by everyone. So y' never admit that school could be anythin' other than useless.

(FRANK ***passes her the ashtray but she ignores it and continues sharpening the pencils on to the table.***)

RITA Like what you've got to be into is music an' clothes an' lookin' for a feller, y' know the real qualities of life. Not that I went along with it so reluctantly. I mean, there was always somethin' in me head, tappin' away, tellin' me I might have got it all wrong. But I'd just play another record or buy another dress an' stop worryin'. There's always somethin' to make you forget about it. So y' do, y' keep goin', tellin' yourself life's great. There's always another club to go to, a new feller to be chasin', a laugh an' a joke with the girls. Till, one day, y' own up to yourself an' y' say, is this it? Is this the absolute maximum I can expect from this livin' lark?

Discussion

Think about the ways that Russell shows us the differences between the two characters. Who is in charge here? Think about the **setting** (Frank's room at the university), the topics of conversation, and the way they both speak.

He has attempted to differentiate between the two characters in a number of ways. Think about what they are:

Rita	*Frank*
Readin' an' studyin'	Reading and studying
I don't wanna reform y'	You think you've reformed me
She said I was off me cake	What in the name of God is being off one's cake?
an' that's not allowed.	By whom?

The differences are not simply in the way that Russell shows us how Rita actually says her words, but in the choice of the words, and the word order. Frank is more grammatically 'correct', though this possibly sounds a little pedantic or pompous. 'By whom' is perhaps not a normal part of speech. Rita shortens her words, elides them – 'want to' becomes 'wanna'. She uses slang like 'off me cake', and not only does Frank not understand the expression, he also says 'off one's cake' which does sound pretty incongruous.

Russell isn't suggesting that Rita's non-academic speech means that she is stupid. She is presented as lively and funny, and Frank may seem a little stuffy in comparison, though he obviously enjoys her humour. One of the obvious sources of humour in the play, and in fact the focus of the plot, is the huge difference between the two characters, and the ways in which they change each others' lives.

Extract B

Here is an extract from *Death of a Salesman* by Arthur Miller (1949). In this extract from the beginning of Act 2 of the play, the 'salesman' of the title, Willy Loman, has gone to see his boss, Howard, a much younger man. Willy, exhausted, wants to change his travelling job for one based in New York, where he lives. Howard is preoccupied with his 'wire-recorder' – an early tape recorder – and instead of listening to what Willy has to say, insists on him listening to recordings he has made of his family.

HOWARD The first one is my daughter. Get this. (***He flicks the switch and 'Roll out the Barrel' is heard being whistled.***) Listen to that kid whistle.

WILLY That is lifelike, isn't it?

HOWARD Seven years old. Get that tone.

WILLY Ts, ts. Like to ask a little favour if you ...

(***The whistling breaks off, and the voice of HOWARD'S daughter is heard.***)

HIS DAUGHTER 'Now you, Daddy.'

HOWARD She's crazy for me! (***Again the same song is whistled.***) That's me! Ha! (***He winks.***)

WILLY You're very good!

(***The whistling breaks off again. The machine runs silent for a moment.***)

HOWARD Sh! Get this now, this is my son.

HIS SON 'The capital of Alabama is Montgomery; the capital of Arizona is Phoenix; the capital of Arkansas is Little Rock; the capital of California is Sacramento (***and on, and on.***)

HOWARD (***holding up five fingers***) Five years old, Willy!

WILLY He'll make an announcer some day!

HIS SON (***continuing***) 'The capital ...'

HOWARD Get that – alphabetical order! (***The machine breaks off suddenly.***) Wait a minute. The maid kicked the plug out.

WILLY It certainly is a –

HOWARD Sh, for God's sake!

HIS SON 'It's nine o'clock, Bulova watch time. So I have to go to sleep.'

WILLY That really is –

HOWARD Wait a minute! The next is my wife.

(*They wait.*)

HOWARD'S VOICE 'Go on, say something.' (*Pause*) 'Well, you gonna talk?'

HIS WIFE 'I can't think of anything.'

HOWARD'S VOICE 'Well, talk – it's turning.'

HIS WIFE (*shyly, beaten*) 'Hello. (*silence*) 'Oh, Howard, I can't talk into this ...'

HOWARD (*snapping the machine off*) That was my wife.

WILLY That is a wonderful machine. Can we –

HOWARD I tell you, Willy, I'm gonna take my camera, and my bandsaw, and all my hobbies, and out they go. This is the most fascinating relaxation I ever found.

WILLY I think I'll get one myself.

HOWARD Sure, they're only a hundred and a half. You can't do without it. Supposing you wanna hear Jack Benny, see? But you can't be at home at that hour. So you tell the maid to turn the radio on when Jack Benny comes on, and this automatically goes on with the radio ...

WILLY And when you come home you ...

HOWARD You can come home twelve o'clock, one o'clock, any time you like, and you get yourself a Coke and sit yourself down, throw the switch, and there's Jack Benny's programme in the middle of the night!

WILLY I'm definitely going to get one. Because lots of time I'm on the road, and I think to myself, what I must be missing on the radio!

HOWARD Don't you have a radio in the car?

WILLY Well, yeah, but who ever thinks of turning it on?

HOWARD Say, aren't you supposed to be in Boston?

WILLY That's what I want to talk to you about, Howard. You got a minute? (*He draws a chair in from the wing.*)

HOWARD What happened? What're you doing here?

WILLY Well ...

HOWARD You didn't crack up again, did you?

WILLY Oh, no. No ...

HOWARD Geez, you had me worried there for a minute. What's the trouble?

WILLY Well, tell you the truth, Howard. I've come to the decision that I'd rather not travel any more.

HOWARD Not travel! Well, what'll you do?

Question 1

How does this dialogue reveal to us the relationship between the two men?

Commentary

Let's break this question down into separate parts:

How interested does Howard seem in Willy?

Not very! He pays much more attention to his 'wire-recorder' which is a new toy for him. Possibly Miller is trying to make us think that he doesn't want to confront

Willy, that he is evading the issue. But he is certainly totally preoccupied with his recorder, to the exclusion of anything else.

How much does Howard understand about Willy's life and feelings?

Not much! He tells Willy, who is desperate for money, that he 'can't do without' a recorder. And when he refers to Willy's work, he says: 'You didn't crack up again, did you?' but it is clear that his worry is for the business, not Willy. He wonders why Willy doesn't have 'a radio in the car'. It is clear that he doesn't intend to offer Willy another position with the firm since he asks 'Well, what'll you do?' when Willy says he'd rather not travel. He talks about 'the maid' as if he assumes Willy must have one too.

Who is the dominant partner here?

Howard, who interrupts Willy, constantly, and allows the older man little time to talk. Willy has to bring his own chair in 'from the wings' since he has not been invited to sit down. We also hear Howard on the tape ordering his wife around.

Question 2:
How does the writer present this relationship to us dramatically?

Commentary

When you look at this second question, you are not just thinking about the content of this sequence, but the way the two men have to speak and behave. Consider the following questions:

- Who speaks longer?
- Who interrupts?
- Who asks questions and who answers?
- Who initiates topics of conversation?
- Who orders or instructs?
- Who is more confident and who more hesitant?

Look at these words taken from Willy's speech:

- 'Like to ask a little favour if you ...'
- 'It certainly is a –'
- 'Can we –'
- 'And when you come home you ...'
- 'Well ...'
- 'No ...'

All of these show us points at which Willy is hesitant or is interrupted by Howard.

Another point is the fact that the stage is dominated by the 'wire-recorder'. The setting has only a desk, a chair and the recorder, so the audience's attention, like Willy's, is focused on it. It dominates the stage. But the audience knows that Willy has gone to see Howard in a spirit of optimism. It is likely that the optimism was ill-founded, but the **contrast** and **juxtaposition** make the scene more poignant. We see Willy's hopes of a desk job in New York are simply unattainable, and in the **context** of the whole play, we realise that his death is becoming inevitable.

By drawing attention to the recorder, and showing us the power inequality, Miller has presented his ideas and his characters **dramatically**. Think what would be lost if this scene were not acted out, but simply read.

We will return to this extract towards the end of the chapter when we look at ways of answering a question on a play.

Extract C

Now contrast this extract from the first part of *Waiting for Godot* by Samuel Beckett (1956). All we know is that the two characters are on 'a country road', there is a tree, and it is 'Evening'. They spend their time 'waiting for Godot' who, of course, never arrives. They are very much concerned with the passing of time.

ESTRAGON Charming spot. (***He turns, advances to front, halts facing auditorium.***) Inspiring prospects. (***He turns to Vladimir.***) Let's go.

VLADIMIR We can't.

ESTRAGON Why not?

VLADIMIR We're waiting for Godot.

ESTRAGON (***despairingly***). Ah! (***Pause.***) You're sure it was here?

VLADIMIR What?

ESTRAGON That we were to wait.

VLADIMIR He said by the tree. (***They look at the tree.***) Do you see any others?

ESTRAGON What is it?

VLADIMIR I don't know. A willow.

ESTRAGON Where are the leaves?

VLADIMIR It must be dead.

ESTRAGON No more weeping.

VLADIMIR Or perhaps it's not the season.

ESTRAGON Looks to me more like a bush.

VLADIMIR A shrub.

ESTRAGON A bush.

VLADIMIR A –. What are you insinuating? That we've come to the wrong place?

ESTRAGON He should be here.

VLADIMIR He didn't say for sure he'd come.

ESTRAGON And if he doesn't come?

VLADIMIR We'll come back tomorrow.

ESTRAGON And then the day after tomorrow.

VLADIMIR Possibly.

ESTRAGON And so on.

VLADIMIR The point is –

ESTRAGON Until he comes.

VLADIMIR You're merciless.

ESTRAGON We came here yesterday.

VLADIMIR Ah no, there you're mistaken.

ESTRAGON What did we do yesterday?

VLADIMIR What did we do yesterday?

ESTRAGON Yes.

VLADIMIR Why ... (***Angrily.***) Nothing is certain when you're about.

Commentary

How is this different from the extract from *Death of a Salesman*? You can see here that there is little attempt to distinguish between the two characters. Their dialogue is more or less interchangeable. If anything, they seem to resemble a pair of Music Hall comedians, exchanging repartee.

Look at the question below, which is based on an AQA B sample paper.

Question

How does Beckett make waiting into something dramatic and theatrical?

You should find it helpful to know that the paper from which this question comes is targeted at AO2 and AO3 only.

So, you are being asked to show your **knowledge and understanding**, and to focus on **how writers' choices of form, structure and language shape meanings**. As in the extracts we have previously examined, the focus is still on the **generic** qualities of the passage – the fact that it is drama, and that you need to be aware of its **theatrical** possibilities.

For example, look how quickfire the exchanges are. On a bare set, with no trappings of character, the writer has to engage the audience's interest in what happens on stage. We can see that in a way the dialogue between the two characters goes nowhere. There is little sense of a **linear** plot. A linear plot is one which progresses via a series of stages or changes to a distinct conclusion or **closure**.

Beckett is writing in a particular way – what has been referred to as 'absurdist'. The setting and characterisation are not **realistic**, nor is the dialogue. The two characters are speaking in an odd way. It is almost as if their dialogue proceeds independently, as if neither is listening to the other. (But think about the ways in which this is different from Howard not listening to Willy.) Yet they do understand one another too. For example, they don't name the 'he' they talk about, but they both know who 'he' is.

Beckett is concerned with the ways people try to make sense of the world, in the face of apparent ultimate meaninglessness. One way he can do this is by a kind of bleak, or black, humour. Nothing much changes in the world of *Waiting for Godot*, yet somehow the characters go on existing, always in the hope that something will happen that will make things better.

The **structure** of this play depends on repetition, with two acts in which apparently nothing happens, though in other ways there are some changes. Beckett is partly writing a play about the difficulties of communication in a medium, the theatre, which depends upon communication. His characters are essentially solitary, but the humour arises from the mixture of absurd dialogue, and static situations.

If you are to answer a question on a play such as this, you need to discuss the details of the dialogue within the particular techniques the writer (in this case Beckett) is deploying, and the particular kind of writing this is.

What Beckett is not trying to do is represent realistic dialogues and situations on stage. It would be useful for you to compare the comments on structure and characterisation in Caryl Churchill's *Top Girls* later on in this chapter.

KEY CONCEPTS

closure	contrast	dramatically
generic	juxtaposition	linear
realistic	setting	structure
theatrical		

6.5 Context

AQA A	U3
AQA B	U2
EDEXCEL	U1
OCR	U3
WJEC	U2
NICCEA	U1

Assessment objective 5i (**show understanding of the contexts in which literary texts are written and understood**) is targeted in a number of the exam papers. Let's look now at two extracts from different pre-twentieth-century plays, *The Rover* by Aphra Behn (1677), and *The Rivals* by Richard Brinsley Sheridan (1775), and see how contexts can be understood and applied. Both of these extracts come from the earlier parts of the plays.

Extract A: *The Rover*

FLORINDA What an impertinent thing is a young girl bred in a nunnery! How full of questions! Prithee no more Hellena; I have told thee more than thou understand'st already.

HELLENA The more's my grief. I would fain know as much as you, which makes me so inquisitive; nor is't enough I know you're a lover, unless you tell me too, who 'tis you sigh for.

FLORINDA When you're a lover, I'll think you fit for a secret of that nature.

HELLENA 'Tis true, I never was a lover yet, but I begin to have a shrewd guess what 'tis to be so, and fancy it very pretty to sigh, and sing, and blush, and wish, and dream and wish, and long and wish to see the man; and when I do, look pale and tremble, just as you did when my brother brought home the fine English colonel to see you. What do you call him? Don Belvile?

FLORINDA Fie, Hellena.

HELLENA That blush betrays you. I am sure 'tis so. Or is it Don Antonio the Viceroy's son? Or perhaps the rich old Don Vincentio, whom my father signs you for a husband? Why do you blush again?

FLORINDA With indignation; and how near soever my father thinks I am to marrying that hated object, I shall let him understand better what's due my beauty, birth and fortune, and more to my soul, than to obey those unjust commands.

HELLENA Now hang me, if I don't love thee for that dear disobedience. I love mischief strangely, as most of our sex do, who are come to love nothing else. But tell me dear Florinda, don't you love that fine *Anglese*? For I vow, next to loving him myself, 'twill please me most that you do so, for he is so gay and so handsome.

FLORINDA Hellena, a maid designed for a nun ought not to be so curious in a discourse of love.

HELLENA And dost thou think that ever I'll be a nun? Or at least till I'm so old till I'm fit for nothing else? Faith no, sister; and that which makes me long to know whether you love Belvile, is because I hope he has some mad companion or other that will spoil my devotion. Nay, I'm resolved to provide myself this Carnival, if there be e'er a handsome proper fellow of my humour above ground, though I ask first.

FLORINDA Prithee be not so wild.

HELLENA Now you have provided yourself of a man, you take no care for poor me. Prithee tell me, what dost thou see about me that is unfit for love? Have I not a world of youth? A humour gay? A beauty passable? A vigour desirable? Well shaped? Clean limbed? Sweet breathed? And sense enough to know how all these ought to be employed to the best advantage? Yes, I do and will; therefore lay aside your hopes of my fortune by my being a devote, and tell me how you came acquainted with this Belvile, for I perceive you knew him before he came to Naples.

FLORINDA Yes, I knew him at the siege of Pamplona; he was then a colonel of French horse, who, when the town was ransacked, nobly treated my brother and myself, preserving us from all insolences. And I must own, besides great obligations, I have I know not what that pleads kindly for him about my heart, and will suffer no other to enter. – But see, my brother.

(Act 1, Scene 1)

Extract B: *The Rivals*

JULIA But what has been the matter? You were denied to me at first!

LYDIA Ah! Julia, I have a thousand things to tell you! But first inform me, what has conjured you to Bath? Is Sir Anthony here?

JULIA He is. We are arrived within this hour – and I suppose he will be here to wait on Mrs Malaprop as soon as he is dressed.

LYDIA Then before we are interrupted, let me impart to you some of my distress! I know your gentle nature will sympathize with me, though your prudence may condemn me! My letters have informed you of my whole connection with Beverley – but I have lost him, Julia! my aunt has discovered our intercourse by a note she intercepted, and has confined me ever since! – Yet, would you believe it? She has fallen absolutely in love with a tall Irish baronet she met one night since we have been here, at Lady Macshuffle's rout.

JULIA You jest, Lydia!

LYDIA No, upon my word. She really carries on a kind of correspondence with him, under a feigned name though, till she chooses to be known to him – but it is a *Delia* or a *Celia*, I assure you.

JULIA Then, surely, she is now more indulgent to her niece.

LYDIA Quite the contrary. Since she has discovered her own frailty, she is become more suspicious of mine. Then I must inform you of another plague! That odious Acres is to be in Bath today; so that I protest I shall be teased out of all spirits!

JULIA Come, come, Lydia, hope the best Sir Anthony shall use his interest with Mrs Malaprop.

LYDIA But you have not heard the worst. Unfortunately I had quarrelled with my poor Beverley, just before my aunt made the discovery, and I have not seen him since, to make it up.

JULIA What was his offence?

LYDIA Nothing at all! But, I don't know how it was, as often as we had been together, we had never had a quarrel! And, somehow I was afraid he would never give me an opportunity. So, last Thursday, I wrote a letter to myself, to inform myself that Beverley was at that time paying his addresses to another woman. I signed it your *Friend unknown*, showed it to Beverley, charged him with his falsehood, put myself in a violent passion, and vowed I'd never see him more.

JULIA And you let him depart so, and have not seen him since?

LYDIA 'Twas the next day my aunt found the matter out. I intended only to have teased him three days and a half, and now I've lost him for ever.

JULIA If he is as deserving and sincere as you have represented him to me, he will never give you up so. Yet consider, Lydia, you tell me he is but an ensign, and you have thirty thousand pounds!

LYDIA But you know I lose most of my fortune, if I marry without my aunt's consent, till of age; and that is what I have determined to do, ever since I knew the penalty. Nor could I love the man, who would wish to wait a day for the alternative.

JULIA Nay, this is caprice!

(Act 1, scene 2)

Both plays are concerned with the position of women in society, and both are comedies, though *The Rover* is rather darker in its mood and concerns.

Question:

How significant do you think it is that *The Rover* is written by a woman?

Commentary

The extract is the beginning of the play, and it immediately raises issues of the treatment of women in its society. I have selected from the text quotes that show:

(a) women being told what they have to do
(b) women showing independence of spirit.

How would you allocate the following quotes to these two categories?

1 'will suffer no other to enter'
2 'the rich old Don Vincentio, whom my father signs you for a husband'
3 'than to obey those unjust commands'
4 'And sense enough to know how all these ought to be employed to the best advantage,

5 'makes me so inquisitive'
6 'I love mischief strangely, as most of our sex do'
7 'I'm resolved to provide myself this Carnival'
8 'a maid designed for a nun'.

I think you will probably agree that category (a) includes quotes 2, 3, and 8. But even in category (a) we can see that quote 3, for example, shows defiance. We can see that Behn differentiates between the two characters. Hellena is more spirited and independent than her sister Florinda. But even though Florinda seems more conventional, she is still resolved not to marry 'the rich old Don Vincentio' and to marry the man of her own choice. She will 'suffer' (that is, to allow) 'no other to enter' her heart.

Behn is clearly identifying these issues of society in her play. Her setting is not England, but she is universalising matters which affect women's lives, as she shows by Hellena's claims about the female sex.

The Rivals, however, seems to explore the trivial nature of women's lives. Sheridan stresses the contrasting nature of the two women who speak very differently. This is of course, a crucial part of **dramatic technique**. (It might be helpful to compare the extract from, and discussion of, *Educating Rita* (see pages 127–128), particularly with reference to Russell's use of contrasting voices.)

The attitudes to love, marriage and women's lives are **foregrounded** in both extracts. Lydia, in Extract B, complains of her treatment by her aunt. Look at the following quotations taken from this extract:

- 'You were denied to me at first'
- 'has confined me ever since'
- 'she is become more suspicious'
- 'you know I lose most of my fortune, if I marry without my aunt's consent, till of age'
- 'now I've lost him for ever'.

If you compare these quotations with those from *The Rover*, there might seem to be a similarity, since the subject of both seems to be the oppression of women. Yet it is clear that Lydia is positively encouraging ill-treatment. She has a falsely romantic view of love, and is deliberately trying to make herself impoverished by marrying against her aunt's wishes. She manufactures trouble between herself and her suitor, the Ensign Beverley, and mocks the romantic hopes of her aunt, Mrs Malaprop. She sees her relationship with Beverley in terms of 'teasing', and Julia's judgement of Lydia's 'caprice' seems a fair one.

Ideas and attitudes

As far as the situation in *The Rover* is concerned, the fact that a woman can be forced to marry someone of their father's choice, or be threatened with a life in a convent against their wishes, is presented to the audience as a real threat which has to be resisted in every possible way. It is in direct opposition to a lively young woman's potential happiness and wishes. It is very likely that the audience will be firmly on Hellena's side in this conflict.

It is possible to like the character of Lydia because of her liveliness and high spirits, but Sheridan is surely not asking the audience to entirely approve of her. The comic tone of the play means that the audience is unlikely to feel that the play will end in unhappiness. The tone of *The Rover*, however, is more threatening. The play includes scenes of attempted rape, and it is difficult for a modern audience to take these as totally comical.

One point that can be made about the ideas and issues in plays is whether the writer ultimately questions or endorses the society they are writing about. We have discussed the way that unequal power is a feature of dramatic dialogue, and you should think about where the writer's sympathies lie, and what he or she is criticising or mocking.

Context summary

As part of the context of the play you are studying, you need to be ready to explore ideas and attitudes towards society as well as personal relationships, and to decide how the writer intends the audience to respond.

You should remember that audience response will change according to period. Our attitudes towards women and rape are likely to be very different from those of audiences in Behn's own time. And, to return to the point made at the beginning of this discussion, the gender of writer and audience may well be important in responding to and evaluating texts. Even 300 years after a play was written, it may strike men and women differently because of the ideas about and attitudes to women it is presenting.

If you think about all of these issues, you will be directly addressing the demands of AO5i, in addition to other assessment objectives which may be targeted.

6.6 Structure

AQA A	U3
AQA B	U2
EDEXCEL	U1
OCR	U3
WJEC	U2
NICCEA	U1

I have referred throughout to the importance of the assessment objectives – and reminded you of them at regular intervals. One problem that students have with AO3 (**show detailed understanding of the ways in which writers' choices of form, structure and language shape meanings**) is their inability to write about structure, and what effect this has on the text as a whole.

In order to apply this idea in particular to drama, let's now turn to one of the set texts, *Top Girls* by Caryl Churchill. There are different ways of examining any text, of course, and we could link this play to the two we have just discussed, in that it concerns women's lives. It has also been seen as very much of its time (1982). A character in it – Marlene – is a symbol of a 1980s career woman. Margaret Thatcher was Prime Minister at the time, and there is a parallel between her and the character of Marlene. So there is a context for it, that is worth exploring. But for the purposes of this section we will be focusing on the chosen structure for the play, which does link closely with its ideas and context.

Structure: general

If you think about the structure of any play, you can make one obvious point about the way in which the writer has split it up. There is considerable variation, from two acts (as in *Death of a Salesman*) to a number of shorter scenes (as in *A Streetcar named Desire*).

It is useful to think about the effects of this splitting, or structuring. At some point there will be a climax in the conflict and some kind of resolution. It is difficult to generalise beyond this, but you need to see how the plot of your text is worked out. It is usually possible to identify a turning point, or points, where the action begins to change. This may be a change in events or in relationships, but drama does depend on change and clashes. Since plot could be defined as the pattern of events and situations in a text, you will realise that the writer's selection of these events and the order in which they are presented is crucial. They are selected and ordered to have a particular effect on the audience.

Structure: Top Girls

In the case of *Top Girls*, Churchill rejects the traditional linear structure of a play. Instead, she moves from one time setting to another, and the women characters' speech is presented more like a piece of music than as part of a plot moving towards a resolution. One point that can be made about this structure is that it could be said to link more to the pattern of women's lives which are perhaps more repetitive than purposeful and goal-directed. This is relevant to the content of the play which concerns itself with the effects of work on women's lives. Churchill has also rejected the idea of realism in the play: Marlene holds a dinner party to celebrate her promotion, and her guests are women who are both historical and mythological figures.

Churchill herself has said that her choice of women was 'fairly arbitrary' and this unstructured creation of character fits in with the rejection of a linear plot – one which works towards a resolution in which the events of the plots and the interactions of the characters fall into place.

One point to notice, though, is that all the characters in *Top Girls* are female. If you are studying this play, you will realise how different this is from most or all of the plays you are familiar with.

The discussion of this play has focused on an overview of the writer's selection of particular kinds of plot, setting and characterisation which are very different from 'traditional' techniques. It is important that you don't overlook these essential features and their effects. Compare the discussion of *Waiting for Godot* earlier in this chapter for development of these ideas.

KEY CONCEPTS

context	linear	pattern
plot	realism	structure

Sample question and model answer

We can now refer back to the extract from *Death of a Salesman* by Arthur Miller which we examined earlier in the chapter (page 129).

Here is a question using this extract as its starting point.

Critics have commented that Miller presents dramatically the pressures of society on ordinary people like Willy Loman. How does he make us care about Willy's fate?

This question targets AO1, as all questions will, AO2 implicitly, AO3 and AO5 directly. AO4 is addressed by use of a critical view. This is a very common way of achieving this particular objective in a question.

Now look at is an answer to this question, which is in effect in two parts. I have extended the original answer, and then commented on why the extension (shown in brackets) is better in terms of the question and the assessment objectives.

Answer

1 the point is clarified and developed
2 a more extended comparison made
3 textual support given
4 comment developed, with reference to the power relations between the two characters
5 extract linked to rest of the play

Miller shows Willy in contrast to Howard [by showing us Howard's financial success in contrast to Willy's poverty **1**]. Howard shows little concern for Willy's problems [and he is too interested in his own life and family to listen to what Willy has to say **2**]. Howard interrupts Willy constantly [for example when he says, 'Wait a minute! The next is my wife. **3**]. He boasts about his own family [and Willy is forced to compliment his son's achievements **4**], saying 'He'll make an announcer some day!' [and the audience is aware that Willy has problems in his relationship with his own son, and is worried about his son's life and career **5**].

6 awareness of genre and literary techniques
7 development and links with whole text
8 textual support
9 more textual support and more movement out to rest of play

It seems that Miller wants to show the audience Howard's materialistic outlook on life [by making them focus on the 'wire-recorder' **6**]. Willy is forced to pretend he has a radio in his car [though we have seen much evidence in the rest of the play that he struggles just to pay his household bills **7**]. Willy, an older man, has to defer to the younger Howard [and Howard shows him little respect: Willy even has to bring his own chair 'from the wings' before he can sit down **8**]. Because the audience knows that Willy is desperate, this makes Howard's indifference even more callous [and when Howard calls him 'kid' later in this sequence, this adds to the sympathy we feel for Willy **9**].

10 terminology used, reference to genre, some awareness of structure, link to rest of play, focus on writer
11 awareness of context

The audience know that Howard is Willy's last hope [and the juxtaposition of this sequence with a more optimistic one presents Willy's plight even more extremely. We know the extent of Willy's desperation since Miller has shown us on stage Willy's memories, and hopes, and fears **10**]. Willy comes to represent all ordinary people who struggle to survive [in the post-war world **11**], and are disregarded by such people as Howard.

In this chapter we have examined a number of extracts from set plays, and focused on different aspects of dramatic techniques. We have applied this analysis to typical exam questions set by different exam boards, and examined the way that the Assessment Objectives can be achieved in your responses. Student answers have been discussed in order to demonstrate the most effective ways of analysis, with an emphasis on particular ways of improving your answers. There has been a focus on the use of close detail from the texts, and the importance of genre in terms of dramatic techniques and effects has been central to the discussions.

LEARNING SUMMARY

Exam practice and analysis

[Closed Book]

Question

Death of a Salesman (Arthur Miller)

To what extent do you think the play marginalises female characters?

AOs targeted: AO1, AO2i, AO5i

Notes

The question is Closed Book, so it requires more of an overview. There is a contrast to the last question which required detailed consideration of a particular extract.

AO1: depends on ability to construct a clear and sustained argument with textual reference, appropriate terminology and accurate English.

AO2i:

- an understanding of the structure of the play as a whole with reference to the role played by women
- reference to scenes in which Linda appears
- contrast between Linda and 'the woman'
- what Linda knows and doesn't know
- how she affects Willy
- relationship with her sons
- way she and Willy speak
- possible reference to minor roles of other females.

AO5i:

- need to engage with idea of 'author' and concept of 'marginalised'
- understanding of Miller's implied attitudes
- awareness of context in terms of dramatic genre
- awareness of gender relationships of the period and perhaps the way they have changed.

Index

Acknowledgements

The author(s) and publisher are grateful to the copyright holders, as credited, for permission to use quoted materials and photographs. They are also grateful to the attributed Exam Boards for permission to reprint specimen and actual questions.

Short Story on a Painting of Gustav Klimt. Lawrence Ferlinghetti, *City Lights*, USA

No One So Much As You (from Collected Poems), Edward Thomas, *OUP; Professor R. George Thomas and Myfanwy Thomas*

Whitsun Weddings (from Collected Poems), Philip Larkin, *Faber and Faber Ltd*

Waiting for Godot, Samuel Beckett, *Faber and Faber Ltd*

Translations, Brian Friel, *Faber and Faber*

Head of English, (taken from Standing Female Nude), Carol Ann Duffy, *Anvil Press Poetry*

Sheepdog (taken from Voices Off), U.A. Fanthorpe, *Peterloo Poets*

Desert Places (taken from The Poetry of Robert Frost), *The Estate of Robert Frost; ed. Edward Connery Lathem; Jonathan Cape*

Enduring Love, Ian McEwan, *Jonathan Cape*

The Handmaid's Tale, Margaret Atwood, *Jonathan Cape*

A Streetcar Named Desire, Tennessee Williams, *Copyright © 1947, 1953 renewed 1975, 1981 The University of the South; Published by New Directions; Reprinted by permission of The University of the South, Sewanee, Tennessee. All rights whatsoever in this play are strictly reserved and application for performance etc. must be made before rehearsal to Casarotto Ramsay & Associates Ltd., National House, 60–66 Wardour Street, London W1V 4ND*

An Unknown Child (from Pangs of Love) Jane Gardam, *Chatto & Windus; David Higham Associates Ltd*

The Great Gatsby, F. Scott Fitzgerald, *David Higham Associates*

The Color Purple, Alice Walker, *The Women's Press; David Higham Associates*

Knowledge of Angels, Jill Paton Walsh, *Transworld; David Higham Associates*

Snow Falling on Cedars, David Guterson, *Bloomsbury Publishing plc*

Regeneration, Pat Barker, *(Viking, 1991) copyright ©Pat Barker, 1991; Penguin UK*

The Devil's Disciple, Bernard Shaw, *The Society of Authors, on behalf of the Bernard Shaw Estate*

Educating Rita, Willy Russell, *Methuen*

Every effort has been made to trace copyright holders and to obtain their permission for the use of copyright material. The author(s) and publisher will gladly receive information enabling them to rectify any error or omission in subsequent editions.